# COMPLAINTS
## of the Saints

Blessings ~
the Crabby Mystic
S. M. Lea Hill

# COMPLAINTS
## of the Saints

## STUMBLING ON HOLINESS
## WITH A CRABBY MYSTIC

### BY MARY LEA HILL, FSP

BOOKS & MEDIA

Boston

Library of Congress Control Number: 2019952634
CIP data is available.

ISBN 10: 0-8198-1683-3

ISBN 13: 978-0-8198-1683-2

Every effort has been made to trace copyright holders and to obtain their permission for the use of copyright material. The publisher apologizes for any errors or omissions and would be grateful if notified of any corrections that should be incorporated in future reprints or editions of this book.

Cover design by Dan Wegendt

Published by Pauline Books & Media, 50 Saint Pauls Avenue, Boston, MA 02130-3491

Printed in the U.S.A.

www.pauline.org

Pauline Books & Media is the publishing house of the Daughters of St. Paul, an international congregation of women religious serving the Church with the communications media.

1 2 3 4 5 6 7 8 9                    24 23 22 21 20

*To our founder, Blessed James Alberione, who said,*
*"It makes me rejoice when one of you brings me a book*
*that you have written. I offer it immediately to God."*

*and*

*In loving memory of*
*Father James (Jim) T. Edwards, Jr.*
*1950–2020*
*Saint Louis, Missouri.*
*The best of priests and a person who never needed this book.*

# Contents

A Monk's Tale . . . . . . . . . . . . . . . . . . . . . . . . . . . *xiii*

Acknowledgments . . . . . . . . . . . . . . . . . . . . . . . . *xv*

Introduction . . . . . . . . . . . . . . . . . . . . . . . . . . . . *1*

### Part I

### Complaints and Their Causes

1. Lamentability . . . . . . . . . . . . . . . . . . . . . . . . . *7*

2. Complaints Are Common . . . . . . . . . . . . . . . . . *9*

3. Why We Complain . . . . . . . . . . . . . . . . . . . . . . *11*

4. Both/And . . . . . . . . . . . . . . . . . . . . . . . . . . . . *13*

5. Normal People . . . . . . . . . . . . . . . . . . . . . . . . *15*

6. Oops! . . . . . . . . . . . . . . . . . . . . . . . . . . . . . . *17*

7. Learned Behavior . . . . . . . . . . . . . . . . . . . . . . *19*

8. Ease, If You Please . . . . . . . . . . . . . . . . . . . . . *21*

9. My Genes Are Too Tight . . . . . . . . . . . . . . . . . *23*

10. Compliance . . . . . . . . . . . . . . . . . . . . . . . . . . *25*

11. Porcupines . . . . . . . . . . . . . . . . . . . . . . . . . . *27*

## Part II

## Complaints of Some Saints

12. Definition of a Saint (Saints and Aints) . . . . . . . . . . . . . *31*

13. Why Pray to the Saints? . . . . . . . . . . . . . . . . . . . . . *33*

14. Guess Who Complained . . . . . . . . . . . . . . . . . . . . *35*

15. Jesus, Too! . . . . . . . . . . . . . . . . . . . . . . . . . . . . . *39*

16. Standards . . . . . . . . . . . . . . . . . . . . . . . . . . . . . *41*

17. Holy Equality . . . . . . . . . . . . . . . . . . . . . . . . . . *43*

18. Contemporary Complaints . . . . . . . . . . . . . . . . . *45*

19. First Love . . . . . . . . . . . . . . . . . . . . . . . . . . . . . *47*

20. Three Ts . . . . . . . . . . . . . . . . . . . . . . . . . . . . . . *49*

21. La Madre Says . . . . . . . . . . . . . . . . . . . . . . . . . . *51*

22. Lisieux . . . . . . . . . . . . . . . . . . . . . . . . . . . . . . . *53*

23. Saint Thérèse and the Rosary Banger . . . . . . . . . . . . *55*

24. Poorest of the Poor . . . . . . . . . . . . . . . . . . . . . . . *59*

25. Patron Saint of Complainers . . . . . . . . . . . . . . . . . *61*

26. How Paul Did It . . . . . . . . . . . . . . . . . . . . . . . . . *65*

27. Leper Priest . . . . . . . . . . . . . . . . . . . . . . . . . . . . *67*

28. Brother Leo's Complaint . . . . . . . . . . . . . . . . . . . *71*

29. Divine Mercy . . . . . . . . . . . . . . . . . . . . . . . . . . . *73*

30. Domestic Holiness . . . . . . . . . . . . . . . . . . . . . . . *75*

31. Saintly Doppelganger . . . . . . . . . . . . . . . . . . . . . . *77*

32. There's Nothing to Do! . . . . . . . . . . . . . . . . . . . . *79*

33. What a Disappointment . . . . . . . . . . . . . . . . . . . . *81*

34. Why Am I So Unlovable? . . . . . . . . . . . . . . . . . . . . . *83*

35. Blown Call . . . . . . . . . . . . . . . . . . . . . . . . . . . *85*

36. Holy Mountain . . . . . . . . . . . . . . . . . . . . . . . . *87*

37. Moving Men . . . . . . . . . . . . . . . . . . . . . . . . . . *91*

38. Thanks for Asking, Saint Gertrude . . . . . . . . . . . . . *93*

39. Dear Diary . . . . . . . . . . . . . . . . . . . . . . . . . . . *97*

40. "Since Thou Dost Love" . . . . . . . . . . . . . . . . . . . *99*

## PART III

### Complaints from the Holy Book

41. Red Flags . . . . . . . . . . . . . . . . . . . . . . . . . *105*

42. Too Heavy for Me . . . . . . . . . . . . . . . . . . . . . . *107*

43. Complaining Prophet . . . . . . . . . . . . . . . . . . . . *109*

44. Where Were You? . . . . . . . . . . . . . . . . . . . . . . *111*

45. Complaint Inside a Complaint . . . . . . . . . . . . . . . *113*

46. Two Men Walk Into . . . . . . . . . . . . . . . . . . . . . *115*

47. Front for Faults . . . . . . . . . . . . . . . . . . . . . . . *117*

48. Trashing . . . . . . . . . . . . . . . . . . . . . . . . . . . . *119*

49. More Trashing . . . . . . . . . . . . . . . . . . . . . . . . *121*

50. In the Beginning . . . . . . . . . . . . . . . . . . . . . . . *123*

## PART IV

### Learning from the Saints How to Handle Complaining

51. Look the Part . . . . . . . . . . . . . . . . . . . . . . . . *127*

52. My Sainted "Other" . . . . . . . . . . . . . . . . . . . . . *129*

53. Statuesque. . . . . . . . . . . . . . . . . . . . . . . . . . . . *131*

54. Truth Be Told . . . . . . . . . . . . . . . . . . . . . . . . *133*

55. Wishing Well . . . . . . . . . . . . . . . . . . . . . . . . . *135*

56. Terrible News . . . . . . . . . . . . . . . . . . . . . . . . . *137*

57. Imperfect Perfection . . . . . . . . . . . . . . . . . . . *139*

58. Perfect Imperfection . . . . . . . . . . . . . . . . . . . *141*

59. Facial Recognition . . . . . . . . . . . . . . . . . . . . . *143*

60. Life Vision . . . . . . . . . . . . . . . . . . . . . . . . . . . *145*

61. Two Who Could Have . . . . . . . . . . . . . . . . . . *147*

62. Alberione's Advice . . . . . . . . . . . . . . . . . . . . . *149*

63. Little Conversations . . . . . . . . . . . . . . . . . . . . *151*

64. Super-Duper Hero . . . . . . . . . . . . . . . . . . . . . *153*

65. Saints and Complaints . . . . . . . . . . . . . . . . . . *155*

66. Daily Challenge . . . . . . . . . . . . . . . . . . . . . . . *157*

Characteristics of Charity . . . . . . . . . . . . . . . . . . . *159*

   I. Charity is patient . . . . . . . . . . . . . . . . . . . . . *160*

  II. Charity is kind . . . . . . . . . . . . . . . . . . . . . . . *161*

 III. Charity does not envy . . . . . . . . . . . . . . . . . . *162*

 IV. Love is not pretentious . . . . . . . . . . . . . . . . . . *163*

  V. Love is not puffed up . . . . . . . . . . . . . . . . . . *164*

 VI. Love is not ambitious . . . . . . . . . . . . . . . . . . *165*

 VII. Love is not self-seeking . . . . . . . . . . . . . . . . . *165*

VIII. Charity is not provoked . . . . . . . . . . . . . . . . . *166*

 IX. Charity thinks no evil . . . . . . . . . . . . . . . . . . *168*

  X. Charity doesn't rejoice over wickedness (injustice) . . . . *169*

XI.   Charity rejoices with the truth . . . . . . . . . . . . . . . *170*

XII.  Charity bears all things  . . . . . . . . . . . . . . . . . . *171*

XIII. Charity believes all . . . . . . . . . . . . . . . . . . . . . *172*

XIV.  Charity hopes all things . . . . . . . . . . . . . . . . . . *173*

XV.   Charity endures all things . . . . . . . . . . . . . . . . . *174*

XVI.  Reading from First Corinthians . . . . . . . . . . . . . . *175*

Postscript . . . . . . . . . . . . . . . . . . . . . . . . . . . . . . *179*

Notes . . . . . . . . . . . . . . . . . . . . . . . . . . . . . . . . . *181*

# A Monk's Tale

The young monk had a vow of silence. Once a year his superior asked how things were going.

The first year he replied: "Food's bad."

The next year he said: "Bed's hard."

The third year he commented: "Chapel's cold." Then he added simply: "I quit."

"And it's a good thing," his superior said, "because for three years all you've done is complain."

# Acknowledgments

Scripture quotations noted in this book are taken from the following:

*New Revised Standard Version Bible: Catholic Edition,* copyright © 1989, 1993, Division of Christian Education of the National Council of the Churches of Christ in the United States of America. Used by permission. All rights reserved (NRSV).

*The New Testament: St. Paul Catholic Edition,* translated by Mark A. Wauck, copyright © 2000 by the Society of St. Paul, Staten Island, New York, and are used by permission. All rights reserved (TNT).

Scripture texts in this work are taken from *The Holy Bible: Contemporary English Version,* copyright © 1995, American Bible Society, 1865 Broadway, New York, NY 10023, and are used by permission (CEV).

Scripture texts from the book of Psalms are taken from *The Psalms: A Translation from the Hebrew,* translated by Miguel Miguens, copyright © 1995, Daughters of St. Paul. All rights reserved. Used with permission (MP).

# Introduction

You may be tempted to ask why another book on the saints? At which point I would be tempted to retort: is that a complaint?

Holiness is an activity open to everyone. Of course, it is no secret that saints have problems *and* saints can *be* problems as well.

We have all read books about saints who appear to be made of plaster of paris. Not that these saints were mere statues, but they never moved out of their holiest poses. We never saw their humanness, what made them so like us. We saw their heroism, their holiness, but not their humanity. Biographers were simply overzealous by attempting to make the saint's halo shine brightly as an exemplar of all things virtuous.

For many readers, myself included, this type of writing is off-putting. It's not that someone couldn't have lived such a stellar life, but since that isn't our experience, the accounts fail to teach us anything useful. Certainly, we admire the saints, but we don't have much incentive to imitate someone presented as confirmed in virtue because we aren't starting from a level playing field. While they progressed straight through every obstacle, we keep spinning our wheels on the road to perfection. Therefore, I've decided to write about saints from the perspective of their faults in order to observe their steps toward victory.

This book will not be a defense of our personal defects, but rather a celebration of our successes. We want holiness, but we also want our own way. We really are the "children" of God with so many whims and wants that get in the way of God's plans for us.

With this in mind, let's focus on the tendency to complain. Why do we care if we have complainers around? They are just annoying for the most part. If we ourselves are the complainers, however, it should be concerning. First and foremost because Jesus tells us we are to be holy, in fact, as perfect as the heavenly Father (see Mt 5:48). And complaining just doesn't seem all that perfect. The mandate to be perfect may appear a bit steep, but it's simply this: to try to love God with our whole mind, will, and heart, and love our neighbor as ourselves.

I don't know about you, but it bothers me that I complain. It tells me that my personal program of life is not in sync with Jesus' program. So, the next best step is to try making some sense of the whole wide world of complaints. What better way to go about this than to take a look at how certain saints dealt with complaints? Which saints complained? Isn't it a bit of a scandal to even admit that they might have complained? And, what would saints have complained about?

True confession: I chose the topic of complaints because it's the area I'm most familiar with. It is an expression of my own character, which explains my tagline: The Crabby Mystic. I am a crabby person called to holiness. I can also attest to the fact that when we are on a personal quest for holiness (as we all should be), enlightenment often comes from something we stumble upon rather than from years of prayer and reflection. So I invite you to join me to see what this all meant to the saints and what it can mean for you and me.

## PART I

# Complaints
# and Their Causes

# 1

# Lamentability

Words can be a problem. For example, how often do I have to check myself on whether to use *compliment* or *complement* in a sentence? The dilemma is the same for *anecdote* and *antidote* or *laid* and *lied*. I remember being called up to my teacher's desk in second or third grade because I had chosen incorrectly between *come* and *came*. I tried arguing that it was difficult to tell the difference between them, but the teacher suggested that I study better.

> "When *I* use a word," Humpty Dumpty said, in rather a scornful tone, "it means just what I choose it to mean—neither more nor less."
>
> "The question is," said Alice, "whether you *can* make words mean so many different things."
>
> "The question is," said Humpty Dumpty, "which is to be master—that's all."[2]

And when it comes to arguments and complaints, like Humpty Dumpty, we do intend that our word usage is the *master meaning.*

The choice of words, their meaning, their usage, and the ensuing arguments are also leading contributors to the fine art of complaint. There had to have been an original kerfuffle, of course, but how words are used and how they are understood can quickly lead us down the path of confrontation.

Not all complaints are created equal. They come in all shapes and sizes and exist for all sorts of reasons. Basically, a complaint expresses dissatisfaction with something that is wrong, unfair, or unacceptable. Dictionaries tell us that the root of complaint is from the Latin *complangere,* meaning "*lament.*" We can see this in the word *plaintive*, as in a *plaintive cry*, or from a *plaintiff's reaction*. From this we realize that many complaints are just laments that things are not better.

One of the most common causes of complaint is annoyance. We all get annoyed, even infants. Think of your reaction when suddenly a baby starts wailing while you are delayed in a grocery store line or a medical office waiting room. "Thank you," you mumble, "I was just about to say the same thing."

Complaints can also stem from misunderstanding, embarrassment, pettiness, pride, aggravation, and, sometimes, simply mean-spiritedness.

A word similar to *complaint* is *compliant*. We don't like to be simply *compliant,* but how do you think *complaint* can become a more positive dynamic in certain circumstances?

# 2

# Complaints Are Common

Why get annoyed to the point of complaining? It's because something isn't right, and I cannot rectify it outright. For any variety of reasons, a direct confrontation isn't possible. I'm not the right person; it's not the right time or place; perhaps I'm not even sure of the motivations for this "wrong" that needs "righting." In any case, a complaint seems to be the best weapon of righteousness available to me.

These samples from convent life can illustrate what I mean.

A complaint could be a snide, indirect response to someone's overzealous comment about my food consumption.

*Her:* "Why are you always eating donuts? You shouldn't eat them, especially those fancy ones!"

*Me:* "Not to worry! I know a plain donut is better for you than a frosted one—so I licked all of the chocolate off before I ate it."

*Translation:* Stop harassing me about my health!

Some complaints are just meant to be entertaining (hopefully) as this one from Sister Carmela, a notoriously creative person and plain-spoken individual: "The Church should change the prayer for the dead. How can they enjoy eternal rest if a perpetual light is on?"

Here's another example of a common complaint: "*Why don't you affirm me more?*"

Once a sister complained like this to Mother Thecla Merlo, the co-foundress of the Daughters of Saint Paul, my religious congregation. "Mother," she said, "Why do you only see and correct the wrong things that I do? You never tell me how well I am doing." Mother Thecla replied: "God sees and rewards what we do well, but my job is to help you become better."

How often do we complain *because* others are doing their duty?

Not all complaints are negative, and they can appear in various forms, such as statements, questions, or recommendations. We've all heard this one: *"If you're cold, put on a sweater."* There's also this one: "*Wasn't it cold in the house this morning!*" Or this one: "*What's the use of a furnace if we never turn it on?*"

Saint John Henry Cardinal Newman explains:

> It is the characteristic of our minds to be ever engaged in passing judgment on the things which come before us. No sooner do we apprehend than we judge: we allow nothing to stand by itself: we compare, contrast, abstract, generalize, connect, adjust, classify: and we view all our knowledge in the associations with which these processes have invested it.[3]

Newman is referencing our natural thought processes. Do we also have a natural responsibility to channel our thoughts so that the outcome will be realistic and genuine?

# 3

# Why We Complain

A complaint is often a valid observation that we might not have the virtue to convey appropriately. I like to think of complaints as social commentary. This way they have more class and become a more dignified way of saying what needs to be said (to no one in particular, but everyone in general). In the matter of complaints, we hold to very biased views. We side with the opinion closest to our own, so they are often "our own" by default.

What do we complain about? Here are a few scenarios:

— Someone offended me;

— I am living in fear;

— I can't get ahead;

— People are mean;

— I am weak, addicted, impatient, hopeless, etc.;

— My spouse ignores me;

— Authority targets me;

— I'm losing my edge: I'm forgetful, tired, disinterested, etc.;

— I've been cheated, robbed, offended;
— Life isn't fair;
— I can't pray; I can hardly believe.

Am I at the point that I complain *because* I complain? Why was I born with this disposition? Why not sweet, accepting, excusing? Why do I burn to comment and complain? What does all this mean?

— Does complaining become a habitual recourse?
— Is it my feel-good response?
— Is it so automatic that I can complain without engaging reason or even will?
— What can I do to be more authentic about my perception of wrong?

The real crux of complaining is not what is said, not the effect, but the intent in saying it. Am I just blustering, just making a comment for comment's sake, making a joke, or is my intention something negative, insidious, hurtful, or downright evil? Sometimes we later assign a more positive intention after seeing the pain or confusion our complaint caused, but wouldn't it be better if we kept an eye on our intentions so as to be better prepared when the urge to complain arises?

———— ✳ ————

A helpful prayer:

Let my words and my thoughts be pleasing to you, LORD, because you are my mighty rock and my protector. (Ps 19:15 CEV)

Write a short prayer from your own heart.

# 4

# Both/And

*"So then, if you complain, you aren't a saint? It's that simple!"*
Is it really? What about all the other human faults and failings that we don't label as serious sins? Complaining is just a part of the catalog of common defects we all draw from. Think, for example, of a white lie, a broken promise, a personal slight, an act of impatience, a small dishonesty, etc.? Can we be saints with these minor millstones around our necks?

Some failings are seen as more disastrous and damning than others, such as hatred, bodily harm, corruption, or perversion. While none of these failings offers portraits of holiness, by contrast complaints may only tarnish our haloes.

*"We're working on these things. We're getting the upper hand and soon we'll be free of all faults, failings, sins. And we'll be saints!"*

So then, is being human an impediment to being a saint? We could be martyred, then that final heroic act will do the trick. But, for most of us life is more complicated, and *we* are more complicit in our daily actions and reactions. Above all, however, we keep in mind that God's grace is more infusive than we can imagine. God is always pulling for us, egging us on to side with virtue, inspiring us with the best ways to respond.

Once a pious man complained to his rabbi: "I've worked so hard and diligently served the Lord, but have not improved. I'm still just an ordinary, ignorant man."

The rabbi replied: "At least you now know that you are ordinary and ignorant, and this is a great accomplishment."

So then, the first best step would be to acknowledge that we do complain. Next, we need to find out why, and last, what can we do about this habit of complaining.

So let us speak of complaints *and* saints. These two are not mutually exclusive; they do not cancel each other out. Saints were people like us who became holy. There is nothing magical about holiness. It is the work of a lifetime. It comes from God's grace blessing our human effort. Holiness is the goal of life for each one of us. Standing between us and our goal, however, are our defects. In *Complaints of the Saints* we will discover how even our defects can lead to holiness.

Think of something about yourself that you'd like to improve. What do you imagine will be a good strategy for turning this into virtue?

# 5

# Normal People

What do normal people do?

One Sunday on my way to an unfamiliar parish, I was looking for the sign. A car was closely following me, and we were traveling at a nice clip. This particular church is set quite far in from the street in a property of trees and lawns. It has a large marker much like those calling attention to estate housing. Suddenly I spied the sign and needed to make a quick turn, but I feared that the other car would hit my fender. So I sped up and turned sharply into the next driveway, which happened to lead to a diocesan facility. The car following me turned into the driveway too. I pulled over quickly and impatiently waved the car on, while hoping that it was not the bishop or a priest we know, and then I u-turned out.

What would a normal person do when a car innocently kept them from an expected, though sudden, turn? I suspect such a person would calmly say: "Uh, oh. We're going to have to turn around." That's all. No fuming, no irritation, no thought of having been offended.

What a waste of energy, both physical and spiritual! Every day is a step forward and two backward, then twirl and begin again. This is the normal pattern of the recovering complainer.

Of course, I should be working more intently on my dispositions, but I dare say God does his part so graciously. He jumps in with a kindly reprimand as soon as I relax my ire and then guides me through some reflection on my failed virtue. God does expect prayer and new effort, but never throws in the towel on me. If God can't have my good graces on the first trip out, he will meet me on the u-turn.

What we complain about is one thing. Why we complain about it is another. What we'll do about complaining is another matter still. What are your thoughts?

# 6

# Oops!

How often we hear this advice when preparing for confession: *"Don't keep bringing up your past sins."* There are a couple of good reasons for this. The first is the most important: our sins have been completely removed by the absolution we received from the priest. They are gone! The second reason is stated wisely by Saint Antony the Abbot: "Do not revisit old sins lest the war be renewed upon you."[4] In other words, don't invite back the temptation that led you to sin. We should never presume that we are strong enough to prevail the second time if we failed so easily the first time. God forgave the sin; he didn't change our natural impulses. Yes, the sacrament of Reconciliation strengthens us for the future, but we don't want to burn our bridges by playing with fire.

Some things do require remembering. One of these is the humiliation we feel when we realize that a judgment we leveled on someone or something was totally unjustified. If we look closely at these judgments, they are, more often than not, just another way of placing a complaint.

There are always things to complain about. Here is one of my less-embarrassing complaints. One evening I may have been the only one of a community of thirty-five in chapel who secretly grumbled about the candles. Why were there four candleholders and only two candles? Now my recollection was ruined! What possessed the sacristan to place candles only in the back holders? Everything looked off kilter. Next morning when I entered chapel for Sunday Eucharist, I gazed at the altar and the liturgical *faux pas* had not been rectified. Perhaps I could inconspicuously go up there and put the two candles in the front holders. But as I hesitated, the organ began to play signaling the start of the entrance procession. As we sang, I lovingly looked at the crucifix leading the procession and noticed that it was flanked by two sisters each carrying a candle identical to the two in the stands by the altar. And, yes, these two additional candles made their way to the empty holders. Now all is well, all is complete. And I, the master complainer, have once again come up empty, possessing only lost energy and smoldering embers of complaint.

Have you ever found yourself revisited by a past mistake? What is your strategy for regaining your peace?

# 7

# Learned Behavior

Do complaints have a relationship to anger? In her book, *Thoughts Matter: The Practice of the Spiritual Life*, Mary Margaret Funk tells us that although we console ourselves by assuming that anger is basically uncontrollable, it is rather a learned behavior that can be unlearned.[5]

Sometimes when we recognize anger in ourselves, we just accept that we are persons prone to anger. We don't believe the tendency is correctable. And, we believe that if it is learned behavior, there is no way to escape being angry (or at least being angered). "It's who I am," we say. Perhaps I grew up with an angry parent or lived with an angry spouse. They may have expressed their anger in complaints and it rubbed off on me. I learned the same behavior. So, of course, we would willingly claim, "It's not my fault."

What shall we say? Often our anger comes out in complaints. And this too is a learned expression of anger. How many events and circumstances of life, big and small, cause anger to simmer in our soul? Are we justified? Humanly speaking, maybe we are. As Christians, however, it is our duty and our *privilege* to model ourselves on the behavior of our Savior. Who would have had more reasons to be angered, considering how he was treated by those he came to save?

But, speaking of learned behavior, Jesus instructed us, "*Learn of me* for I am meek and humble of heart."

This means constantly translating offense to offering, insult to invitation, hurt to heart. We have to train ourselves to move from negative to positive every time. This is more likely if we do not nurse what hurts us, what insults us, what offends us. Make yourself invent excuses for those who earn your wrath. Then after this, make sure you don't allow a complaint to escape. It can happen that while we are congratulating ourselves for not striking out, we might leave an unguarded crack that allows a complaint to slip out. The danger of this is that we hear our complaint, and this emboldens our injured ego, and we may feel the impulse to add another one or two *innocent* little complaints. If the person we are aiming at is no more virtuous or prepared than we are, a little verbal battle of complaints and insults may ensue. Like the opening salvos of a tennis match—nice and easy at first, then high-powered bursts.

How would you go about helping someone unlearn this behavior?

# 8

# Ease, If You Please

It is hard to imagine life before electricity or batteries. Nowadays some people even prefer voice commands to pushing buttons. But back in *the* day (several lifetimes ago), cranks were a convenience. Cranks made life pleasurable. Great-great (*maybe another-great*) Granddaddy's car would sputter to life after a vigorous cranking of the motor shaft. Fresh, lye-scented laundry was cranked through rollers to wring out the water before hanging it out to dry. Even a delectable cup of home-made ice cream came from a hand-cranked churn. Activating the phone on the wall required cranking the handle a few times to get the operator's attention.

So, in the mechanical realm cranks were both useful and well-loved. In our music-loving culture we often hear a call to "crank it up"—raise the volume so we can enjoy the song even more.

What we won't hear is a call to crank up our complaining. But that is what we are doing when we indulge our propensity to complain; we are allowing ourselves to devolve from being a complainer to being a crank.

When I think of cranks, I think of "Mr. Gizmo" whose driveway abutted the back side of our house. We were known affectionately as "little monsters." To Mr. Gizmo we were simply annoying. We imagined that he worked in a quiet office perhaps in banking or insurance, but then at home he had to endure the pack of noisy kids next door. Mom and Dad strongly advised us to stay away from the fence that separated the two yards, but we often "forgot," as the excuse goes. In any case, there were never any reciprocal invites to backyard barbecues.

I imagine the German word for hospital—*Krankenhaus*—has some relation to our word cranky that connotes some sort of illness, perhaps a physical problem or an illness of the spirit. We, who are crabby/cranky, fantasize that we are not usually that way. Something happened to cause this temporary "illness" to come over us. It is true that some kind of dyspepsia of the spirit can from time to time cloud our vision, but if you are often accused of being a cranky crab, it's time for an examination.

Think about times you have caught yourself cranking up your complaint about this or that. Are you dealing mostly in annoyances or is there an underlying issue? Take your discovery to prayer, and then, if you feel the need, talk to a trusted friend.

# 9

# My Genes Are Too Tight

Do you think complaining is a simple, personal fault—as innocent or guileless as snoring? "*It just happens,*" we say. And perhaps there is some truth to that on a surface level. "*It is a matter of personality, of genetics, of training, even the result of physical or emotional pain*"—all things beyond our control. And beyond our control only in origin—they did not originate with me, so I leave it at that and say therefore I can't do anything about it. "*It's not my fault*"—is not just a cop-out, but a denial of my free will. It means I have no control of destiny or daily life, and I don't want to be seen so weak.

We have control, even if it is only over our efforts. We may not succeed in changing this aspect of our character; the merit will be in *trying* to change. There is nothing meritorious in doing nothing. Christ so much as said this in the parable of the master handing out money before a journey (see Mt 25:14–30). The story involves three men. One receives an amount that he doubles; the second gets less, but likewise doubles it. The third buries what he received and makes no profit. He was cast out, while the other two received appropriate rewards on an equal basis according to their individual effort.

And surprise! Or not! The saints were very real people—perhaps as real as it is possible to be, which means they had defects or shortcomings. They were holy not just despite their defects, but actually, and to a certain degree, *because* of their defects.

You are, no doubt, looking askance at my words. You are questioning how holiness and defects work together. Let's look at ourselves a moment. What brings you to prayer? Isn't it often your less than stellar performances? In other words, your defects motivate you to pray. And this coming to prayer despite your defects is an indication that you possess a certain degree of humility.

Here is a very short prayer to keep handy when defects and shortcomings seem to be gaining the upper hand. Humility is so welcome by our Lord.

"Lord, I am not worthy."

"Lord, I have sinned again."

"Lord, have mercy."

# 10

# Compliance

Some among us go through life relying on the same excuse or complaint, such as, "The dog ate my homework." They apply this to nearly every questionable situation. But what if we get to heaven and find that our dog actually made it, too? Our much-relied on cover will be blown.

Another way of complaining is by not complying. An example of this would be the folks in the Acts of the Apostles (see 5:1–11) who sell property to benefit the Church. First the author of Acts praises the community for their oneness of spirit and their sharing of the Word and worldly goods. Then he tells us about a husband and wife who say they are complying, who want to appear as a true brother and sister along with the other generous contributors. They said they were offering the entire proceeds of the sale of property for the common good, but withheld part of the sale price for themselves. They were not complying with this new policy as the others had, but were actually registering a complaint against "company policy." They were pretending to be pious.

A very dramatic story unfolds as the husband and wife were confronted individually with their farce as they approached Peter. First he said to the husband: "You lied to God, not just to men." Then when the wife came with the same faulty story, he said to her: "Why did you agree to test the Spirit of the Lord?"

The conclusion: "And great awe came over the whole church and all who heard these things," as we can well imagine. It may seem a bit unfair of God to have them both, husband and wife, die for something that really should have been voluntary. The beginning of the Church, however, was an extraordinary time. They were in miraculous days. But the big problem was that this couple lied to the Holy Spirit practically right after the Spirit had brought the Church to birth at Pentecost. For all we know, they might have been present in the Upper Room among the many disciples.

Our takeaway here has to be the importance of truthfulness. Yes, even in the area of complaints. Let's ask ourselves if we have ever tried to make an excuse by lying. If we have a complaint, let's at least present it truthfully.

# 11

# Porcupines

Mother Thecla Merlo observed:

Wherever we go we always bring ourselves, the baggage of our defects, our self-love which always wants to dominate, and so we are unhappy. Unhappy because there is that person. If only there were another!

There are some who are like porcupines; as soon as they are touched they prick you, and no one wants to stay with them. But the fault is always someone else's.[6]

Why would someone be so hard to endure? Really, the examination of motives belongs to the "porcupine." Unhappiness generally expresses itself. It cannot remain silent. Even if no words are said, the actions and attitudes complain. The annoyance becomes obvious, but the reason for it can only be sought within the heart of the complainer.

Complaints never just appear from nowhere. They are not isolated entities. There is always a "why" to be discovered, to be befriended, to be accepted or gently dissolved. Ranting, accusing, striking out are no more helpful than cowering, whimpering, and hiding when it comes to what causes complaint. Because we don't always have control over what causes us to complain, we need to develop a strategy for dealing with whatever raises our ire. Begin by honestly telling yourself why you had to complain (this will require some soul-searching). Then try to make peace with it: either there is some truth to it (however small) or it is a fabrication, something we imagined or misunderstood, and so the best approach is to admit it to yourself. Then smile at yourself for making such a big story out of next to nothing. Turn it into a prayer, a little conversation with God.

The very insightful Benedictine, Dom John Chapman, offers this approach:

> So you will get detachment from *things* and from *self*, by merely giving yourself to God, and *accepting yourself* as you find yourself to be. We all have one unpleasant person to live with, whom we can't get away from—ourself. Put up with yourself, and take your own hated imperfection and weakness as an unpleasantness you have to bear with. It is very hard, but it is really a very perfect act of love to God.
>
> I daresay this won't help you. God is leading you all the time. The only fault will be if you are restless, and want to do something of your own. Let God do it.[7]

The secret here is to let God do it. How much do I trust God with my personality?

PART II

# Complaints
# of Some Saints

# 12

# Definition of a Saint
# (Saints and Aints)

In spiritual terms there are two kinds of people: the saints and the *aints*. Either someone is a saint or they aren't. Every single person who is in heaven is a saint. And all of us on earth have the potential. A process is available to each of us. To help us match our individual potential to that necessary process, there are no better teachers than the saints who have gone before us *and* those saints who still live among us.

The New Testament calls all believers "saints." So, from the day of our Baptism, this is our official designation, our identity, unless we mess up and repudiate the grace of our redemption. Some of us will be recognized as exemplary, and our saintly designation will be capitalized. We'll have the Saint before our names. The majority, however, will always be lowercase saints. This is not a slight to our dignity in any way. We, too, will be saints. The fact is that God makes some saints more obvious in their lifetimes so that they can show us the way to holiness. The Church canonizes these holy people so we can remember them throughout the centuries, learn from their example, and continuously praise the goodness of God who is the giver of all grace.

The distinction between the canonized and uncanonized saints is similar to the setup of the Church's liturgical year: every day of the year is holy, but some are feast days, celebrated with great solemnity. Most days are simply part of Ordinary Time, but each day celebrates the same great mystery of our redemption.

Blessed James Alberione often said, "You don't become a saint *after* you die. It is the work of a lifetime."

Then we retort, *"We thought you said that holiness is not done by us, but by God. So why talk about the work of a lifetime?"*

Both are correct because we have to spend our lifetime cooperating with God's grace.

In one of his homilies, Saint John Paul II told us that holiness is not to be measured by our human norms. It is, in fact, not reserved to an extraordinary group of people but is available to everyone. God makes us holy if we join forces with him to save the world. Not even our sinful and rebellious character will hold us back.

# 13

# Why Pray to the Saints?

Most of us do pray to the saints—to our favorites, for example:

Saint Gerard for childbearing;
Saint Michael for the Church;
Saint Joseph for essentials;
Saint Dymphna for mental health;
Saint Thérèse for simple wisdom;
Saint Christopher for travels;
Our Lady for *everything!*

We pray to saints for holy stuff, but how about for holi*ness*?

For example: if you pray to Saint Christopher when you get in your car, is it just for physical safety? You say: "No accidents, please." But, instead, or in addition to this, do you ever ask Christopher to pray *for* you? "Dear Saint Chris, you carried the Christ Child to safety across a raging stream, pray for me today as I step into the rivers of my life. Keep me steady, clear-sighted, cautious, calm, and brave. And, let me see the needs of others traveling beside me; make me a Christ-bearer, as you were. Oh, and no accidents, please."

We ask Mary to pray for us every time we say a Hail Mary: *"Pray for us now and at the hour of our death."* That encompasses every moment of our lives from right now until God calls us home. What would she not help us with? What would she not obtain for us? What would she not protect us from? The question is, however, are we *really* asking her to pray for us or are we just reciting the words?

So it is with every saint and blessed. Saints are exemplars of so many virtues and intercessors in so many needs. We look to saints as positive role models. They also offer cautionary tales in the life of virtue.

As the title of this book invites, we are looking at the saints who model for us the very human flaw of complaining and ask for their counsel.

If complaining isn't your thing you will have to read in place of it whatever your difficulty is, that is, anger, impatience, pride, prejudice, laziness, laissez-faire attitude, vanity, etc. I think, however, we all indulge in some complaints. It is one of the most common and most obvious problems we can have. It is also a vent for many deeper issues.

It is a fact that saints complain, but that begs the question: What do they complain about and why? It is shocking enough to hear that holy people complain, but we try to imagine what could tick off a saint. How much different would their complaints be from our own?

# 14

# Guess Who Complained

Let me surprise you a little by stating that even our Blessed Mother complained. Yes, she did. Think about the scene in Luke 2:41–52. The Holy Family, Joseph, Mary, and their twelve-year-old son Jesus had gone to Jerusalem to celebrate the Passover. On the return journey, Mary and Joseph realized that Jesus wasn't with either of them. They checked around among family, friends, and traveling companions, but with no success. Their only choice was to retrace their steps to Jerusalem. Saint Luke says that it took three days to locate Jesus. It appears he was lost—ON PURPOSE!

They found him in the Temple surrounded by a group of teachers discussing the Law. Relieved after that frantic search, Mary addresses her complaint to Jesus: "Son, why did you do this to us? You see your father and I have been looking for you, worried to death!"

Having seen mothers in action, I don't imagine Mary was in her most serene state at this moment. She is not reciting a line from a rosary reflection pamphlet; this was the real-life moment when parents reunite with a lost child. Jesus, at twelve, was old enough to be scolded for not considering his parents' feelings. Mary had every (parental) right to say her words more emphatically than we might imagine she should. And, although Scripture doesn't record any words from Joseph, we can imagine he was having words with one or more of the teachers present.

Mary complained to her Son for not consulting them about his decision to stay behind, for giving his parents such a fright, and, perhaps also, simply for growing up too soon.

My point in beginning with Mary is to illustrate that complaining is a *perfectly* natural human reaction. Mary, as we Catholics believe, was conceived without original sin, which means that throughout her entire life she never offended God (or neighbor) by sin. She was, however, a human being. Because she was not touched by sin, she did not have any of the disordered reactions that the rest of us have. She displayed in this Gospel incident a good anxiety, very natural and proper to the situation. We would have been taken aback if she had simply said something terse, like, "There you are! Come on, we're going home." No, we are grateful to be able to *feel* the moment with her, to *experience* her motherly heart.

Another very poignant example of Mary's humanness is the incident where she and other relatives have arrived at a house where Jesus is preaching. Their presence is announced: "Your mother and your brothers are standing outside, wanting to speak to you." Certainly Mary can hear her son's reply as he points to his disciples: "Here are my mother and my brothers! For whoever does the will of my Father in heaven is my brother and sister and mother" (Mt 12:47–50 NRSV). We would not be wrong to imagine that those words caused a twinge in her heart, a very natural desire to utter a complaint, but she doesn't. This, she may think, is a part of the piercing of her heart that the old priest, Simeon, mentioned when Jesus was presented in the Temple.

Mary's heart naturally suffers all the common wounds of motherhood, but she puts her trust in the mysterious plan of God to which she gave her generous, young "yes" (see Lk 1:26–38).

Note other Gospel incidents that might have sparked both human *and* holy reactions from those involved.

# 15

# Jesus, Too!

It is not out of line to point out that Jesus, the God Man, also had occasion to complain, actually several of them (about disciples who didn't understand his words or who couldn't stay awake for one hour's watch with him, etc.). Just imagine one small instance as he is traveling along the road with the Twelve, and he can hear the muffled sounds of conversation. Suddenly, their voices rise, he glances back and they fall silent. When they reach their destination, Jesus faces them with a complaint, "What were you arguing about back there?" (see Mk 9:33). Undoubtedly, he knew, but he was displeased and dismayed that these men who had chosen to follow him day and night were not getting his message. They had been wrangling over which of them was the most important. To put everything in perspective again, Jesus wrapped his arms lovingly around a child and drew him into their midst, saying: "*This is how you should follow me, with the simplicity of a child.*"

Not long before this incident, Jesus had come upon a crowd surrounding his disciples. A man had brought his son, possessed by an evil spirit, hoping for a cure. "I asked your companions to cure him, but they were unable to do so." Jesus responds in absolute frustration: "O unbelieving generation! How long will I be with you? How long will I put up with you? Bring the boy to me." Jesus questioned the father about his son's condition. The man concluded his plea by saying: "If you can, please help us!" Jesus cries out: "*If* you can! Anything is possible if you have faith!" Totally startled by Jesus' outcry and then by the boy's complete cure, the disciples asked Jesus why they weren't able to expel the evil spirit. He replied that it could only be done by prayer.

Imagine yourself in these scenes. How would you reassure Jesus of your devotion and your seriousness in following him? Can you identify those feelings in your life with Christ today? Or, are you perhaps the one complaining that following Jesus is too difficult in our present society?

# 16

# Standards

Are modern saints less virtuous, or have we lowered the standards of holiness? Neither is true. The saints' biographers are becoming more honest, or more *real*, in their accounts. In the past it seemed that authors of saints' biographies honed in on three dominant themes: the saint was a miracle worker, a visionary, or a flawless perfectionist. This is why we were more apt to set the saints up on pedestals to admire than to ask them to accompany us on our life journey. A famous spiritual maxim says that "grace builds on nature." We need to see examples of how a saint is made. What in their nature supported the grace they received? And how does this translate into our lives?

Perhaps Vatican II's stress on the universal call to holiness has made us reflect on the need to show that we can become holy because God works with us as we are. To be saintly, we do not need to have every iota of our life perfectly in place. Holiness, as Saint Paul says, *is to be worked out* (see Phil 2:12).

To underscore how our holiness is built on our nature and how we are always under construction while on this earth, we need to ask a question: who was holier—the apostles who were able to miraculously speak many languages at the Holy Spirit's prompting on Pentecost, or Saint Noel Chabanel or Saint Rose Philippine Duchesne, who were missionaries but could never learn the language of the people to whom they were sent?

Saint Noel Chabanel (1613–1649) had a notable career as a Jesuit professor in France but willingly went as a missionary to the Hurons in Canada. Despite great expectations his complaint was his inability to communicate well enough to be effective. To overcome his discouragement, he vowed to stay until his martyrdom.

Saint Mother Duchesne (1769–1852) also came from France to work in the missions in the United States. But she was stymied both by church politics and her struggles to learn English. In her elder years, Mother Duchesne went to an Potawatomi mission in Kansas but was unable to do anything but pray because she couldn't learn the native language either.

Have you ever lobbied for something and then found you were unable to succeed? Did you complain, blame, or thank God for the opportunity and humbly contribute what you could? Describe your reaction.

# 17

# Holy Equality

Do all saints come out equal? I mean, do they achieve the same degree of sanctity no matter how they became saints? This is a very human question. No one wants to receive the short end of the stick, but holiness isn't something measurable in that sense. Would we say that someone like the Good Thief, whom tradition has named Dismas, would have sanctity equal to Saint John the Evangelist, the young disciple of Jesus who lived to a very old age? How would we determine which one was more of a saint? John labored for years, was exiled, survived attempted martyrdom, cared for Jesus' Mother, wrote one of the four Gospels and perhaps the Letters of John, while Dismas led a dishonest life and was dying as a condemned criminal.

Dismas was inspired to speak to Jesus as they hung together in crucifixion. He seized on the one last grace offered and was rewarded with what amounts to canonization. Jesus told him, "I say to you, this day you will be with me in Paradise" (Lk 23:43 RSV).

Individual holiness is best described by Pauline Martin, Saint Thérèse's older sister, when Thérèse asked this very question about who was holier in heaven. Pauline filled to the top both a glass and a thimble. You can't say one is fuller than the other because both have as much as they can hold. It's not the size or the amount, but the willingness to receive that is the measure.

Reflect with Frank J. Sheed on this topic of nature and grace:

> At the risk of wearying, it must be repeated that grace alone is not the answer. We often deceive ourselves by trying to make the supernatural do the work of the natural, and falling into despair because it does not. We multiply Communions against a particular temptation, and often enough the only result is to increase the strife within us without producing the virtuous act or preventing the sin. The charity of God troubles us, but does not seem to aid us. Once we have grasped the real nature of the struggle, we shall be in no danger of being led by it to despair, least of all to despair of the supernatural, because the supernatural was never promised for that purpose.[8]

So aside from a miracle, which we should not expect here, what is required is this: "The direct work upon our nature has to be done, as we have seen, with labor and pain."[9]

What is your personal strategy for working toward holiness?

# 18

# Contemporary Complaints

In our time, we are able to observe more of the human traits of a saint than was possible in ages past, and it makes their correspondence with grace stand out more startlingly. Let's look at an example of a countercultural saint and her poignant complaint. Jean Donovan (1953–1980), born into privilege in Connecticut, attended prestigious schools and was a successful young woman in the corporate banking world. She is one of those untitled saints who offer us an example of a contemporary saint's complaint. Although Jean is considered by some as merely an unfortunate murder victim, we must note that she was living the life of a saint (total availability to Christ in his people).

As Jean reflected on her next best step in life, she felt a call to be a missionary. She put her life on hold and signed up with a lay missionary team from the Diocese of Cleveland. Ultimately, she would preach the Gospel by serving the suffering kingdom of God in a very troubled region of the world. She was assigned to El Salvador during the bloody civil conflict.

After just a month in the small town of Libertad, observing and sharing the poverty and fear of the people, Jean Donovan wrote these words to one of her friends:

> I keep getting very frustrated and wonder what I am doing here as opposed to being married and living at lollipop acres. . . . Sometimes I'll think: Oh, my God, I'm twenty-six years old, I should be married; I shouldn't be running around the way I am . . . And then I sit there, and I talk to the Lord, and I say, "Why are you doing this to me? Why can't I just be your little suburban housewife?" And you know, God hasn't answered me yet. I don't know. Sometimes I get mad at God. Sometimes I tell God I'm going to chuck the whole thing. I've had it.[10]

In the end, Jean always returned to her original conviction: "There are lots of times I feel like coming home. But I really do feel strongly that God has sent me here, and wants me to be here, and I'm going to try to do my best to live up to that."[11]

She was martyred along with three companions—Sister Ita Ford, MM, Sister Maura Clarke, MM, and Sister Dorothy Kazel, OSU—on December 2, 1980.

What do you think makes a normal young person, like Jean Donovan, invest so completely in the demands of the Gospel? What does the Gospel demand of you?

# 19

# First Love

When I was young, I read *The Story of a Soul*, the autobiography of Saint Thérèse of Lisieux, and I was smitten. I spoke to my father about my admiration for Saint Thérèse. Surprisingly, he said, "Forget about her. She was a saint from the age of three. You *can't* imitate that!"

Was he implying that he knew for a fact that *I hadn't been a saint from the age of three?* Or, was he suggesting that I find a more suitable patron, someone with a more relatable life story?

To my delight, I discovered as I read about her further that Saint Thérèse was much more human than she is given credit for being. We will touch on what that means in a later chapter.

We each need to find the lives of real saints, not to excuse our own weakness, but to encourage our efforts. Over the years, authors have tried to venerate the saints by writing their stories as though the saints lived only from one virtuous incident to another. There is no suggestion that they might have tripped over their own human weakness or offered anything less than a heroic response. Of course, they would have had *to grow* in virtue. There must have been real-life happenings between the holy events that have been recorded. Didn't the saints ever sit down and say, "For heaven's sake, is it really worth it to always be the *good guy*? Why can't I just once snap back at my annoying brother or sister?"

If nothing else, if they didn't have to struggle it would prove my Dad was right that Saint Thérèse *was confirmed in grace and thus inimitable.* But as we read Saint Thérèse's autobiography, letters, and last conversations, we find that her honesty on the topic of holiness is refreshing.

Before saying more about the "little" Thérèse, we will look at the other Teresa, the great Carmelite reformer, Saint Teresa of Ávila. From beginning to end, her story was much more eventful than that of the young girl who finished out her whole life in twenty-four hidden years. Their stories read one like a sweet tableau and the other like the storming of a castle. Both lost their mothers at a young age and both suffered a mysterious, debilitating illness. Beyond that, how different were these two women with the same name.

One of the secrets of sanctity is that the great are also little, and the little are also great. How does this apply to saints you know?

# 20

# Three Ts

Let's talk about the two great Ts: Saint Teresa of Ávila and Saint Thérèse of Lisieux. Along with them, we will look at the third T that is Saint Teresa of Calcutta. These three are among the most popular woman saints of all time, and they demonstrate three of the most common causes of complaints we all run up against: *irksome inconvenience, domestic irritation, and divine silence.*

Let's start with Saint Teresa of Ávila (1515–1582), known to the Carmelites as *La Madre* because of her pivotal role in the reform of that religious order. Teresa was often ill, suffering especially from migraine headaches, but she persevered with the project of renewing the primitive (stricter) observance of Carmelite life. She traveled extensively throughout Spain visiting the convents she had founded or reformed. On one of these trips a well-known episode took place. It was a dark and stormy night (that sounds like a Snoopy opening line), and La Madre was traveling in a donkey cart along a very rough and slippery roadway. She was probably thanking God that she had almost reached her destination when suddenly the predictable happened: the cart slipped off the roadway surface and over-turned into a big patch of mud. Getting to her feet, Teresa found she was unhurt, but she was messy and mortified, and somewhat out of sorts. Indignantly she asked, "Was that really necessary?" The Lord gently chided her, "This is how I treat my friends." "Well," Teresa retorted, "it's no wonder you have so few!"

We are tempted to think how audacious to speak this way to Jesus, but we are envious of her daring and her familiarity. This is Teresa of Ávila's biggest gift to us, however. She is the model of personal prayer. Pray as you are, she always counsels us. Speak to Jesus out of your present moment, and if the moment calls for a complaint, give it.

Here is a little prayer composed by Saint Teresa of Ávila known as *Saint Teresa's Bookmark:*

> Let nothing disturb you,
> Nothing dismay you.
> All things are passing,
> But God never changes.
> Patient endurance
> Attains everything.
> Whoever possesses God
> Wants nothing.
> God alone suffices.

Something to reflect on: All that really matters is a good relationship with God. That will only develop, as all of our relationships do, by engaging in conversation (complaints in-cluded). This is genuine prayer.

# 21

# La Madre Says

Saint Teresa of Ávila is one of the best guides to the life of mystical prayer. She is one of only four female Doctors of the Church, and she is one because of her ability to describe the path of prayer from simple vocal prayer through the heights of contemplation. I believe, however, she deserves the title especially for her realistic description of our daily attempts at prayer.

This very day I have consoled myself with our Lord, and presumed to complain to His Majesty in these words : "How is it, my God, that it is not enough for You to keep me in this miserable life, and that I endure it all for Your sake, and that I wish to live where all this trouble is, because I cannot enjoy You, without at the same time eating and sleeping, and transacting business, and conversing with every one; and all this I suffer for the love of You ? You know well, my Lord! How is it that when there is so little time left over to enjoy Your presence You hide from me? How is this compatible with Your mercy? How can the love You bear me allow this? I believe, Lord, that if it were possible for me to hide from You as it is for You to hide from me that the love You have for me would not suffer it, but You are with me and see me always. Don't tolerate this, My Lord! I implore You to see that it is injurious to one who loves You so much."[12]

Another time she stated: "I also observed, that in this way I began to love our Lord the more. To Him I went to complain of all my troubles, and always I came away from prayer with both comfort and new strength."[13]

Some people consider prayer as another subject to be learned. In academic work the aim is always to perfect our form, for example, in English class we learn composition and grammar so that we will perfect our use of the language. In mathematics, we gradually learn how to add 2+2 until we can take on algebra, geometry, and trigonometry. In learning prayer, it is different. We are not storing up and refining our approach, but we are simplifying and familiarizing our hearts with the One who is at the core of our being.

Do you have a go-to prayer for moments of exasperation? If not, adopt as your own Saint Teresa's Bookmark.

# 22

# Lisieux

The second Teresa is Saint Thérèse of Lisieux, often called the Little Flower. In fact, she was similar to the mustard seed Jesus praises in the Gospel (see Mk 4:30–32). Small, but mighty, Thérèse, from her childhood, knew the power of weakness. She was the little one in her family, and she entered the Carmelite monastery at the very young age of fifteen. She knew how to maintain a childlike charm with others, especially in her relationship with God. Thérèse seemed very simple and unassuming, a sister ready for all sorts of household duties, and one who enjoyed writing poems and putting on plays. She was the kind, little one among her sisters, but Thérèse possessed a heroic heart. Her private sacrifices won the conversion of a convicted murderer just before his execution. In spirit she sometimes trudged along mission trails beside her adopted missionary brothers. Most impressive to me was her ability to joyfully, silently endure the many petty annoyances of close, repetitious, daily schedules. This doesn't mean she was robotic or insensitive to suffering. No, let her relate an example:

Another time I was working in the laundry, and while washing handkerchiefs, the Sister opposite me repeatedly splashed me with dirty water. My first impulse was to draw back and wipe my face, to show the offender I would be glad if she would behave more quietly; but the next minute I thought how foolish it was to refuse the treasures God offered me so generously, and I refrained from betraying my annoyance. On the contrary, I made such efforts to welcome the shower of dirty water, that at the end of half an hour I had taken quite a fancy to this novel kind of aspersion, and I resolved to come as often as I could to the happy spot where such treasures were freely bestowed.[14]

We can reflect with Pope Francis:

Christ says: "Learn from me; for I am gentle and humble in heart, and you will find rest for your souls" (Mt 11:29). If we are constantly upset and impatient with others, we will end up drained and weary. But if we regard the faults and limitations of others with tenderness and meekness, without an air of superiority, we can actually help them and stop wasting our energy on useless complaining. Saint Thérèse of Lisieux tells us that "perfect charity consists in putting up with others' mistakes, and not being scandalized by their faults."[15]

# 23

# Saint Thérèse
# and the Rosary Banger

What are you supposed to do if you are a saint and something calls out for a complaint? I'm thinking of Saint Thérèse who often found some habit of a companion to be annoying, for example, constantly banging rosary beads on the wooden pew during silent prayer. This is how we get on one another's nerves. Let's face it: all of us, whether in a convent or out in the world, need this kind of annoyance in order to gain merit. In other words, we accept these small trials to show the Lord that we do love him and our neighbors.

Saint Thérèse most likely didn't see herself as a saint. She was just a young religious trying to please God by living her vocation as best she could. One of the most beautiful examples of Saint Thérèse's virtue was her interaction with an elderly member of her community who was given to complaints and everyone found difficult.

> I remember an act of charity with which God inspired me
> while I was still a novice, and this act, though seemingly

small, has been rewarded even in this life by Our Heavenly Father, "Who seeth in secret."

Shortly before Sister St. Peter became quite bedridden, it was necessary every evening, at ten minutes to six, for someone to leave meditation and take her to the refectory. It cost me a good deal to offer my services, for I knew the difficulty, or I should say the impossibility, of pleasing the poor invalid. But I did not want to lose such a good opportunity, for I recalled Our Lord's words: "As long as you did it to one of these my least brethren, you did it to Me." [Mt 25:40] I therefore humbly offered my aid. It was not without difficulty I induced her to accept it, but after considerable persuasion I succeeded. Every evening, when I saw her shake her sand-glass, I understood that she meant: "Let us go!" Summoning up all my courage I rose, and the ceremony began. First of all, her stool had to be moved and carried in a particular way, and on no account must there be any hurry. The solemn procession ensued. I had to follow the good Sister, supporting her by her girdle; I did it as gently as possible, but if by some mischance she stumbled, she imagined I had not a firm hold, and that she was going to fall. "You are going too fast," she would say, "I shall fall and hurt myself!" Then when I tried to lead her more quietly: "Come quicker . . . I cannot feel you . . . you are letting me go! I was right when I said you were too young to take care of me."

When we reached the refectory without further mishap, more troubles were in store. I had to settle my poor invalid in her place, taking great pains not to hurt her. Then I had to turn back her sleeves, always according to her own special rubric, and after that I was allowed to go.

But I soon noticed that she found it very difficult to cut her bread, so I did not leave her till I had performed this last service. She was much touched by this attention on my part, for she had not expressed any wish on the subject; it was by this unsought-for kindness that I gained her entire confidence. [16]

Thérèse goes on to say that she also took it upon herself to arrange her food. "At the end of my humble task I gave her my sweetest smile"[17] Because of her care, at the younger sister's death, Sister St. Peter believed that Thérèse preferred her to all the others.

Holiness is not in one exercise or another, it consists in a disposition of the heart, which renders us humble and little in the hands of God, conscious of our weakness but confident, even daringly confident, in his fatherly goodness.[18]

Thérèse complained and was the recipient of complaint. Recall events in your life that are similar. Recall the disposition of your heart at those times.

# 24

# Poorest of the Poor

The third Teresa is Saint Teresa of Calcutta (1910–1997), born Agnes Gonxha Bojaxhiu in Albania. As we know, Mother Teresa founded the Missionaries of Charity who now serve "the poorest of the poor" around the world. In 1928, as a postulant of the Loretto Sisters, she noted whole families living on the street of Madras. If the people back home "could only see all this, they would stop grumbling about their own misfortunes and offer thanks to God for blessing them with such abundance."[19]

Years later while on retreat in 1946, Mother Teresa clearly heard *the call of God* to be a Missionary of Charity. She declared that it came, not as an invitation, but as an order to be accepted in faith. Ever since she said this "yes," God seemed to hide from her.

The whole world imagined that Mother Teresa of Calcutta was enjoying a consoling prayer life, but in fact, it was quite the opposite. With all the good that was being done and all the souls who were brought back to God, God seemed to turn his back on her.

Here is her own description of her inner turmoil:

There is so much contradiction in my soul.—Such deep longing for God—so deep that it is painful—a suffering continual—and yet not wanted by God—repulsed—empty—no faith—no love—no zeal.—Souls hold no attraction—Heaven means nothing—to me it looks like an empty place—the thought of it means nothing to me and yet this torturing longing for God.—Pray for me please that I keep smiling at Him in spite of everything. For I am only His—so He has every right over me. I am perfectly happy to be nobody even to God. . . .[20]

On another occasion in a letter to her spiritual director, Mother Teresa clearly complains of God's abandonment:

Tell me, Father, why is there so much pain and darkness in my soul? Sometimes I find myself saying "I can't bear it any longer" with the same breath I say "I am sorry, do with me what you wish."[21]

Another time Mother Teresa said:

Because I talk so much of giving with a smile, once a Professor from the United States asked me, "Are you married?" And I said, "Yes, and I find it sometimes very difficult to smile at my spouse, Jesus, because He can be very demanding—sometimes." This is really something true. And there is where love comes in—when it is demanding, and yet we can give it with joy.[22]

Think about moments when you were unable to connect with God, when you didn't feel like smiling at God, what did you do?

# 25

# Patron Saint of Complainers

Let's consider the great and eccentric Saint Jerome (331–420), a brilliant scholar who translated the Bible from Hebrew and Greek into Latin. Jerome is best known, fairly or unfairly, however, for his acerbic (biting) tongue. He is literally the poster boy for ill-tempered, dour-faced saints. He was a great critic *and* complainer. I imagine he had qualms of conscience as he translated the letters of Saint James who likened the unfettered tongue to the untamed horse (see Js 3:3).

Jerome also had a thing with skulls. He is almost always pictured with one on his writing desk. Perhaps this solemn posture adds to his mystique. But he must have been patient, kindly, and generous as well, particularly with a certain group of women who considered him a spiritual father. Among them were Saints Paula, Lea, Marcella, Eustochium, and others. Some followed Jerome to the Holy Land to imitate his life of penance and continue studying Scripture with him.

His ornery reputation, on the other hand, is due to a number of bitter sparring matches, mostly over points of doctrine or scriptural interpretations carried on through correspondence.

Fortunately, he did not have access to the electronic devices available today. Here is a tidbit of his that seems made for transmission: "Truth is always bitter, while pleasantness seems to accompany evildoing."[23]

The following are samples of his written complaints.

To a fellow monk from whom Jerome expected some correspondence:

> But since such remissness as yours is never at a loss for an excuse, you will likely declare that you had nothing to write. If this were so, you should have written to inform me of the fact.[24]

Concerning a request to critique someone's writing:

> Let me frankly admit that my indignation overpowers me. I cannot listen patiently to such sacrilegious opinions. . . . But if you wish me to write against him at greater length, send me those wretched dronings of his and in my answer he shall hear an echo of John the Baptist's words.[25]

In defense of his own writings:

> When I want to remove the splinter from my neighbor's eye, I have to cast out the beam from my own eye first. I haven't calumniated anyone. No name has even been hinted at. My words haven't been aimed at individuals and my criticism of shortcomings has been quite general. If anyone wishes to be angry with me, he will have to realize that he himself fits my description.[26]

Indignation over critical comments about himself:

> Some kissed my hands, yet attacked me with the tongues of vipers. . . . One would attack my gait or my way of laughing; another would find something amiss in my looks; another

would suspect the simplicity of my manner. This is the company I've kept for almost three years.[27]

Complaints don't seem to be the special domain of the intelligent or the ignorant. Why do you think complaining is such a level playing field?

# 26

# How Paul Did It

When we consider Saint Paul, we need to start with his personality. Don't you think he had the ideal personality for a complainer? He was proud, intelligent, a man of action, powerful, observant, contentious, well-traveled, direct, and so much more.

"His life," says Blessed James Alberione, "tells us that every temperament can be dominated, corrected, directed, even changed; that Christian character is the result of two elements: prayer and struggle, which even in defeat is a continuous victory; that not only reason and will but also the powers of the heart have to be educated because the heart is a very powerful help, and it's the one that pulls us to God."[28]

It was because of Paul's temperament and his education that Jesus ambushed him on the road to Damascus. Saul was just the man Jesus needed to bring his message to the gentiles. Saul was an observant Jew and yet familiar with the culture and language of the world. Saul's complaint was that this new sect was gaining strength; it was damaging the true faith of the Jews.

Saul had a plan positioning himself at the head of the battle, and God took him seriously. Saul's complaint was heard and clarified. "You are fighting against the goad" (Acts 26:14 CCD). In other words, Saul was pushing against the plan of God so Jesus had to intervene. God couldn't simply drop a flyer in the mail; he had to literally drop Jesus onto Paul's path. Can you imagine Christian history if Paul had found a way to refuse?

Because Paul allowed himself to be turned in his tracks, he was able to follow Christ in a very singular way and offer a model of discipleship. When we are called to even the slightest change of course by God, we are often tempted to balk (another form of complaint). We do not see a reason to think differently, to challenge ourselves, to reach out of our comfort zone. We need the openness of Paul who let his mind be changed, who left himself open to criticism, who switched gears to say "yes" to God.

Our conversions on the journey of life are not often as dramatic as Paul's, but they can be as traumatic. If we always stay on the side of God, remain with his plan for our salvation, and aren't complacent or contrary, we will find God relying on us to carry the Gospel to our world.

Do you grumble at good inspirations that threaten your plans, especially suggestions that come from other people?

# 27

# Leper Priest

Some characters in human history are larger than life. Some are mythical, like Paul Bunyan; others are very real like Saint Damien of Moloka'i (1840–1889). A farm boy from Belgium, the strong, hard-working Jozef de Veuster wanted to give all his energies to God. He joined the Congregation of the Sacred Hearts of Jesus and Mary, received the new name of Damien, and was missioned to the Sandwich Islands, now the state of Hawaii.

In his ninth year there, the bishop asked for volunteers to minister at the leper colony on the island of Moloka'i. Originally only a temporary assignment, Damien spent sixteen years among the lepers. During that time, he worked tirelessly to build homes, educate the children, procure proper food and medicine, pipe in a supply of fresh water, and be priest, medic, and undertaker for his flock.

Father Damien was a man of action, rather rough around the edges, with in-your-face holiness. Although Damien could be difficult, stubborn, and opinionated, after meeting him the author Robert Louis Stevenson described him "with all his weakness, essentially heroic and alive with rugged honesty, generosity, and mirth."[29]

Damien complained of being lonely and abandoned even by his fellow priests; however, those who volunteered to join him had to learn to deal with his irascible character. Meanwhile, because of the publicity he received in the secular press, donations poured in for his work. This often led to disagreements with his superiors and the bishop.

In one such disagreement Father Damien was told to refer the matter to Father Leonor, his provincial superior. To the bishop, Damien had written something to this effect (only notes have been found):

> It is strange! Your Excellency tells me that I have justly won the sympathy of the world. That is expressed by the gifts (975 pounds sterling). My Superiors have only blame for me. From strangers, gold and incense; from my Superiors, myrrh.[30]

Damien also complained about being kept like a prisoner on Moloka'i. He wasn't permitted to travel for fear of contagion. At one point, in frustration, Damien, standing in a little rowboat, yelled his confession up to a priest standing at the rail of another ship. (That was when it paid to know Latin.)

Father Damien possessed a very relatable holiness. He was not living the predictable life of a monk, but a strenuous, stressful ministry among sufferers of one of the most terrifying diseases—a disease he succumbed to himself. He spent himself completely bringing comfort and joy to the abandoned.

When dealing with others, we tend to get bent out of shape by their more obvious defects. How would you assess Father Damien's complaints against the gift of his life?

# 28

# Brother Leo's Complaint

One of the classic Franciscan stories ends in complaints. It was the day of silent preaching by Saint Francis and Brother Leo. "Off we go, Brother Leo," Saint Francis announced. "We're going to preach the Gospel today." They proceeded down one street and up another. They passed the shops and went directly through the center of town, right by the church. Soon they stood before the monastery gate again. Brother Leo, who had been so looking forward to the preaching tour, turned to Saint Francis to complain, "I thought you said we were going to preach. Why, we didn't even greet anyone along the way. Not a word!" Smiling, Saint Francis replied, "We did preach, dear Brother, by our example." This little story is based on a point of the Franciscan Rule that states the brothers must realize that whatever they do is a form of preaching the Gospel.

This rule found life in Tokyo in 1945 when Polish Conventual Franciscan Brother Zeno was noticed walking about the war-ravaged streets. One young woman, a recent convert named Satoko Kitahara (1929–1958) and a Servant of God, was fascinated by this brown-robed outsider as he made his way around the city. She followed him one day and was led down by the river beneath the railroad bridge to the dump. Satoko was amazed to find a settlement among the trash heaps. When Brother Zeno realized Satoko had followed him, he introduced her to the dedicated men who ran what was known as "Ant Town."

Eventually, Satoko volunteered to help with the ragpickers' children. This was fine, but the Ant Town leaders, who were both unbelievers, thought she should be more generous. They complained to her: "If you really believe in your Christ you should live like him. Why don't you give yourself completely?" She accepted this challenge and became a member of the town, living as a (holy) ragpicker until her death from tuberculosis. Her selfless dedication inspired the two Ant Town leaders to embrace the faith, too.

Have you ever been challenged on the basis of your faith to do something more? What did you choose to do and how has it worked out?

# 29

# Divine Mercy

"Loves me; loves me not!" We played this game as children, often while pulling petals off daisies. In her short religious life, Saint Faustina Kowalska (1905–1938) could have been tempted to play it saying, *"Believes me; believes me not!"*

Jesus was asking her to be the apostle of his mercy, but this was not a placid little endeavor. It required suffering, confusion, and lots of humiliation. Why would Jesus treat a dedicated friend that way? She was getting nothing out of this venture. The answer is simple, but no more understandable: when Jesus asks this kind of cooperation, we admire with a tinge of jealousy the visions and messages he grants, but we don't consider that they are often purchased at a steep price. The Lord's trust is a costly gift in this life; glory comes later.

So, we consider Saint Faustina who was believed by some of her companions who supported her with words and prayers, but was seen as odd and exceptional by others. *She must be trying to have it easy and draw attention to herself.*

Imagine a young religious sister sitting on a kitchen table while others much older are working very hard preparing a meal. If you passed by and saw this, what would you be tempted to say to her? Negative comments were made. Faustina, however, was sitting there *in virtue of obedience*. The sister she was working with, Faustina said, "got a little upset with me and, as a punishment, ordered me to sit on the table." That sister's response was overkill, and Faustina admitted, "I thought I'd die of shame."[31]

On another occasion she had gone to speak with her superior about the difficulty she was having making a painting of Divine Mercy that Jesus desired from her. Instead of helpful suggestions, the older sister began screaming all kinds of insults, calling her a faker. How could she deal with such humiliations? She didn't want to complain to her sympathizers at the expense of that cruel superior so she brought these things only to Jesus.

A number of times in her diary, Faustina mentions that she went to complain to the Lord who always explained what he expected her to learn from the experience. He said, "The heart of My beloved must resemble Mine; from her heart must spring the fountain of My mercy for souls; otherwise I will not acknowledge her as Mine."[32]

We all love the devotion to Divine Mercy, but are we only asking Jesus for mercy or are we asking to become merciful? Can you think of an instance when you preferred showing mercy to another at your own expense?

# 30

# Domestic Holiness

It is hard for me to imagine that Saint Zita (1218–1272) never complained. Just look at her life, but even before that look at what she is patron of: housekeepers, maids, domestic workers, waitresses, lost keys, and, I'm adding, stolen fur coats. Aside from the stolen fur coat, a good many women can sympathize with Zita.

Her childhood was normal by thirteenth-century Italian standards, but at twelve she was sent to serve the Fatinelli family in another town. Zita had been well-trained for a life of service and was greatly appreciated by her new "family." She accompanied all her duties with prayer and acts of charity toward the poor. Mr. Fatinelli gave Zita freedom to take from the family's pantries to provide for those in need.

It seems that in everything the Lord had her back. She offered all her prayers and works to him, and he seemed to guarantee all she did. Several examples of this wonderful collaboration involved the miraculous preparation of bread and the recovery of lost keys, but most impressive was the story of the fur coat.

One exceptionally frigid morning, Mr. Fatinelli noticed that Zita was going to the cathedral in a very thin shawl. He offered her the use of his wife's fur coat. When she entered the cathedral, she saw a man shivering in a back pew. She placed the coat over his shoulders saying she would pick it up on the way out. At the end of Mass, however, the man and the coat had disappeared. Terrified, Zita went home and confessed what happened. Of course, Mr. *and Mrs.* Fatinelli were very upset and scolded Zita for her carelessness. Here is where I imagine she might have complained, not to the family, but to Jesus for not watching out for her. One thing we can be sure of is that Zita prayed about her dilemma.

The next morning as she opened the door, to her surprise Zita found the very same man, no longer bent and disheveled, with the coat over his arm. He stepped in without a word and placed the coat in the hands of Mr. Fatinelli, then turned and left. Was it Jesus himself who had borrowed the coat? No one knew, but he truly was watching out for her.

An interesting thought for reflection from Evelyn Underhill: "On every level of life from housework to heights of prayer, in all judgment and all efforts to get things done, hurry and impatience are sure marks of the amateur."[33]

# 31

# Saintly Doppelganger

Caryll Houselander, a twentieth-century spiritual writer, offers us this bit of insight:

> The complaints of discouraged people are never heard on the tongues of the saints; not one of them has ever exclaimed that life had cheated or frustrated him, however much it may have seemed that it had to the onlooker. Circumstances do not frustrate them. Different though they have been in every external detail, there is no saint in Heaven who did not fulfill his human nature on earth.
>
> That which countless millions of unhappy, frustrated people long to achieve and cannot, every saint has achieved, and for every broken human failure, there is a saint like enough to himself to show him his own way to glory.[34]

Not many of us have an identical twin, but we may, one day, discover that we have a doppelganger. Some years back that term was unfamiliar to most of us, but now we see that the media discovers celebrity doppelgangers with amazing frequency. I, for one, fail to see any resemblance in most of these cases, but now I'm happy with the idea of finding a saint who is my spiritual doppelganger. Not only that, but this double will be a guide to (heavenly) glory.

So, who could it be? If I had an addiction to drink, for example, I could turn to Matt Talbot or Saint Monica. If I was looking for a better self-image, I would seek out Saint Mary Magdalene. If I needed help in study, I'd try to imitate Saint Thomas Aquinas. If I suffered racial profiling, I would call on Saint Martin de Porres. Suppose it is a matter of conscience, I would then ask Saint Thomas More or Blessed Franz Jäggerstätter. If I suffer from emotional or mental illness, I'd look to Saint Benedict Joseph Labre or Saint Dymphna. If I wanted inspiration for my married life, I would seek out the help of Saint Gianna Beretta Molla and her husband Pietro Molla, or Blessed Luigi and Maria Beltrame Quattrocchi, the first couple beatified together.

The list of possibilities is endless, but for our purposes here we need saints who can help us maneuver through our propensity to complain. The possibilities here are endless and fascinating. It is good to remember how intertwined complaining is with such human faults as pride, anger, low self-esteem, etc.

What saintly doppelganger would you hope to find? Now, when you become a saint, what will others hope to find in you?

# 32

# There's Nothing to Do!

How often have parents been serenaded by these words: "There's nothing to do"? It is the battle cry of the bored. It was the battle cry of one of the Church's greatest saints. Known to us now as Saint Ignatius of Loyola, Inigo was a soldier seeking adventure, fortune, and glory (the admiration of a beautiful young woman of prominence would also have been welcomed). He suited up in his armor, fastened his sword in place, mounted his noble steed (this all sounds so glorious from our perspective), and galloped off to war. No matter how gallant and heroic the souls of our fighting men and women are, we know that war isn't beautiful or necessarily fulfilling. Yes, the results are what soldiering is all about, but the activity of war is horrendous at best. This was made clear to Inigo soon enough when an enemy cannon ball shattered one of his legs and badly injured the other one. He knew right away this was not something he could easily overcome. In fact, all he could do was lie in agony awaiting capture. The merciful victors, however, brought him to his own country where he eventually recuperated. Unhappy with the look of his newly healed leg, Inigo had it operated on again. This required a longer period in bed. As he felt better, he asked for the popular romance novels of that day. None were at his brother's home where he was. In exasperation he probably let out this too familiar complaint: "There's nothing to do!" Fortunately for Inigo, and all of us, a life of Christ and a volume of lives of the saints were in the house. He devoured them with both his mind and soul, and was captured anew, but this time by the cause of Christ.

His story invites us to read (or view) the same sources and let our soul be captured by the beauty and challenge of following Christ in the footsteps of his saints. Inigo became Saint Ignatius of Loyola, founder of the Jesuits and author of his classic *Spiritual Exercises,* which have helped so many discern God's will for their lives.

If you have been bemoaning the emptiness of your life, Saint Ignatius may be inspiring you to make a retreat with his *Spiritual Exercises* or to read the life of a saint.

# 33

# What a Disappointment

Blessed is he who expects nothing, for he shall never be disappointed.

—Alexander Pope

The older I get the fewer expectations I have about future accomplishments. There simply isn't enough time left for all my great plans. I'm old enough now to accept this fact as a fact. In previous years, however, I fretted and grumbled that my ideas would never be realized. To a certain extent these preoccupations of mine (labeled in my mind as hopes) put a damper on the actual works I was carrying out. In retrospect, these disappointments were of my own making. My first duty was toward what obedience asked of me as a religious.

Of course, I'm not the only person who has been disappointed; it is something quite common and complex. How many people have been disappointed in professional choices, in the place they chose to live, in their parish, the political climate, their education, their children, their spouse, etc.? The list can become endless if we are not careful.

One of the Church's greatest saints died a disappointed man, disappointed but not downcast or defeated. Today he is venerated as one of the greatest missionaries in history. His zeal is legendary. Saint Francis Xavier (1506–1552) was the Apostle of the Indies. He was a wealthy young man bent on a literary career when Saint Ignatius of Loyola began to pursue him with the words: "For what good would it do a man to gain the whole world, but forfeit his life?" (Mt 16:26 TNT)

Francis Xavier joined Ignatius as part of the original core of the Jesuits. He was missioned to India. For the next ten years, he worked tirelessly in India, Malaya, and Japan. Civil officials would not allow him to pursue his dream of entering the vast land of China. Francis didn't have time to mope; instead he hopped a fishing boat with the promise of reaching China. But he was dropped off at the island of Sancian where he contracted a deadly fever. Francis could see China, but died short of his goal. He was only 46 years old. It is said that his dying words were: "In you, O Lord, have I taken refuge, I cannot be disappointed—ever" (Ps 31:1 MP).

Alban Goodier maintains that Francis Xavier's greatest success was in his failure, because in it he resembled the apparent failure of Christ on Calvary.[35] Can you recall a disappointment that brought you closer to Christ?

# 34

# Why Am I So Unlovable?

Do you feel like the center of attention? The whole world revolves around little ole you. Life is amazingly wonderful (and you imagine that you are equally so). That's lovely, but not the sentiment of many, especially as we grow up and become more aware of ourselves and those around us. How many young people—young women for the most part—torment themselves about their looks? Bulimia and anorexia, the classic eating disorders, are so prevalent. Worse yet is the plague of bullying that too often results in suicide. For adults the next step is a surgical procedure to improve their looks. Why go through so much pain and expense? Because I feel unattractive, is the response. *Why am I so ugly and unlovable?*

As they say, let us try walking in the shoes of someone truly unattractive—Saint Germaine Cousin (1579–1601). Germaine was a shepherdess who suffered from terrible growths on her neck caused by scrofula, a bacterial skin disease that attacks lymph nodes. In addition, she had a misshapen arm. Her stepmother banished Germaine to the barn where she slept among the sheep. She was fed scraps from the family's meals, berated, abused, beaten, and worst of all, she felt lonely and unloved. If we even suspected this kind of mistreatment of a child, our immediate reaction would be to call child protective services. Perhaps the neighbors felt pity for Germaine, but they did not intervene.

For her part, Germaine had the greatest respect for her stepmother and often made excuses for her. She did not complain or express any bitterness. In fact, Germaine often gave away the crusts of bread she saved for lunch. Her terrible situation and the constant mistreatment did not embitter her, but enriched her soul. Shortly before her death at the age of twenty-two, a miracle took place that changed things to an extent. Germaine had been accused of stealing bread from the family kitchen. Her stepmother chased her out into the snowy yard and threatened to beat Germaine with a cane if she didn't hand over what she had taken. Unable to escape, Germaine opened her apron, and to the surprise of everyone, instead of the pilfered bread there was a bouquet of fresh flowers. This stunned and dismayed her stepmother. Despite this, Germaine still did not receive inclusion or affection.

Germaine could have, and probably should have, been a classic complainer. How well do you support illness? Do you look for ways to ease the difficulties of the disabled?

# 35

# Blown Call

We are familiar with the idea of a blown call in sporting events. The ump or the ref saw the play one way and called it only to be proved wrong later—often too late to be corrected. And we know the volume of complaints coming from that. In everyday life blown calls also occur from time to time: a date not accepted, a job opportunity overlooked, a car parked too long at a meter, etc. Even saints have had blown calls. The story of Father John Gerard, SJ, is one of these.

Father Gerard (1564–1637) was an English Jesuit ministering covertly in Elizabethan England during the persecution of Catholics. He was extraordinarily successful in hiding his priestly identity from the authorities while carrying on a complex ministry of sacraments and instruction. He would pretend to be a gentleman of moderate means, imitating the life he led before becoming a priest.

When he first arrived in England after his ordination, he was arrested and imprisoned for about a year—not for being a priest but for having no travel permit. When someone posted bond, he had to leave the country. Not to be dissuaded from his mission, Gerard returned clandestinely and managed to serve the underground Church for about eight years until captured. Eventually he was sent to the Tower of London and endured unbelievable torture, even being hung from the prison walls by his hands. He would say nothing about any of the other priests or laypersons he had been working with. Unable to break Gerard's resolve, his captors left him alone in prison.

In 1597, with the help of friends, Father Gerard escaped over the Tower wall on a rope and continued his ministry for a number of years. Then his superior called him to Belgium where he wrote his *Autobiography of a Hunted Priest*. We could imagine that in retrospect Father Gerard regretted not being called to martyrdom as were several of his fellow Jesuits. But he was a very humble man and a very zealous priest who saw in this blown call God's judgment that he was, as he himself said, "unworthy to enter the house of God," and that there was more to be done to strengthen the faith of the Catholics in England.

Think of yourself in Father Gerard's circumstances, not unlike the situation of many persecuted Christians today. Do you think you could be faithful and inventive in following Christ?

# 36

# Holy Mountain

Who is qualified, Lord,
    to take up his abode in your tent,
    to dwell on your holy mountain?
The one who lives uprightly,
    who practices virtue,
    and is truthful to himself.
He does not wander about spreading slander,
    does no evil to his fellows,
    nor does he bring up anything
    to the discredit of his neighbor.
In his eyes a contemptible person is held in disdain,
    whereas he holds in honor those who fear the Lord.
    He takes an oath unfavorable to him, without changing it.
He does not lend his money on interest,
    nor does he accept a bribe to the hurt of an innocent person.
    He who does these things will never alter. (Ps 15 MP)

For a good number of years, I kept a treasured "holy card" in my daily missal. Actually, it was a postcard that I converted to my purposes. The image was the very peak of some mountain. It was a rather garish print job with overly intense blue sky, super white clouds, and gray-green land. Nonetheless, I was pretty attached to that card. On the back I had copied lines of Psalm 15. I got all romantic about the first few lines, but only recently did I realize my neglect of what followed. How many rocks have I dislodged to the detriment of others as I try to climb the Lord's mountain? Especially troubling are the words about a wandering tongue—how often have I brought up things that implicated my neighbor, a practice known as fault-finding or complaining?

Let's quickly bring in Blessed Pier Giorgio Frassati (1901– 1925) of Turin, Italy. He had a motto for his life, *Verso l'alto* "Toward the height"! This is very appropriate on two levels: Pier Giorgio was an avid mountain climber who loved to lead his friends up to contemplate the beauty of nature and enjoy the closeness to God. He told them, "I understand this desire for the sun, to climb high, to go up and find God at the top."[36]

He also ascended the heights in all aspects of life, dedicating his whole day to God's service by prayer and attentiveness to the poor and needy. Everything was done in an unobtrusive way; even his parents didn't realize the extent of his charity. At Pier Giorgio's graduation, his father offered him a car or the equivalent cash. Without any hesitation, Pier Giorgio opted for the money. His father thought Pier Giorgio just wanted to be able to party with his friends. Little did he know that his son spent the money for the necessities of Turin's poor: food, clothing, and medicine. Eventually Pier Giorgio contracted polio on his charitable escapades and died at twenty-four.

The holy mountain of Pier Giorgio was his ascent through the Beatitudes. How would you rate your own spiritual climb?

# 37

# Moving Men

Saint Catherine of Siena (1347–1380) was a woman charged with moving men, very powerful men of history. "Behind every great man there is a great woman," as the saying goes, but in this case the woman had to lead.

This was the time of the Avignon popes, almost seventy years (1309–1377) during which the papacy had taken up residence in southern France rather than Rome. Jesus tasked Catherine, who at this point was a Dominican tertiary and a true mystic, with bringing the papacy back to Rome. In early 1376 she sent several letters to Pope Gregory XI urging him to return the papacy to Rome. She also sent a few of her followers to argue her plan. Finally, she made the trip herself in an effort to be more persuasive. All of this wore on Catherine's strength and her spirit. She sent the following complaint to Pope Gregory:

> Since he [Christ] has given you authority and you have assumed it, you should use your strength and power. If you are not willing to use them, it would be better for God's honor and your own soul to resign."[37]

When Catherine's mother, Lapa, died before having the opportunity to make a confession, Catherine pleaded with Jesus:

> Lord, my God, are these the promises You made to me, that none of my house should go to Hell? Are these the things that in Your mercy you agreed with me, that my mother should not be taken out of the world against her will? Now I find that she has died without the Sacraments of the Church. By Your infinite mercy, I beg You not to let me be defrauded like this. As long as there is life in my body, I shall not move from here until You have restored my mother to me alive.[38]

Along with all her complaints, Saint Catherine has sage advice for Sister Daniella:

> When it seems that God shows us the faults of others, keep on the safer side—for it may be that your judgment is false. Keep silent. And any vice which you ascribe to others, in true humility ascribe to yourself as well. If that vice really exists in a person, he will more willingly correct himself, if he sees himself dealt with gently, and will say of his own accord that which you hoped he would say.[39]

Catherine held Jesus to His promise regarding her family. He did indeed restore her mother to life. Do you have this kind of confidence in Jesus' love for your loved ones?

# 38

# Thanks for Asking, Saint Gertrude

Nothing causes more spiritual angst than seeing your idol fall. Devotees of popular culture deal with this on a daily basis. People search for the shadow side of celebrities and reveal this to the adoring (and disillusioned) crowd.

The book of Daniel describes a larger-than-life figure, a real idol:

> This statue was huge, its brilliance extraordinary; . . . and its appearance was frightening. The head of the statue was of fine gold, its chest and arms of silver, its middle and thighs of bronze, its legs of iron, its feet partly of iron and partly of clay. (2:31–33 NRSV)

We see the weakness right away: heavy components atop *feet of clay* (hence the well-known reference to vulnerability).

How often have we found ourselves looking for some weak point in another's impenetrable perfection? "I really look up to her, but she can't be that good!" When we discover that chink in her splendid armor, we feel either justified or mystified. "I thought she was too good to be true!" Or, "I'm crushed. I never expected that!" Our vision of holiness is either tarnished or turbo-charged.

I want to publicly thank Saint Gertrude (1256–1302), truly Great in my eyes, for boldly presenting this conundrum to Jesus. In her unique relationship with the Lord, Gertrude often had visions and conversations with him. On one occasion, she complained to Jesus about an obvious fault in one of her superiors, whom she greatly admired. Jesus probably gave her one of his loving looks and replied:

> It's not just her, but all of you have some defect. No one goes through life entirely free of them. Why is this? The answer lies in my abundant mercy, tenderness, and love. Your merit is greater in obeying someone whose faults are apparent, rather than only to someone who seems perfect.

Gertrude, never shy of a rebuttal, said: "But, Lord, I am happy to find this in an inferior, but I am adamant about desiring superiors who are free of fault."

To this Jesus replied:

> I, who know all their weaknesses, sometimes permit them, in their diverse ways, to be sullied by some stain, because otherwise they might never reach a very high degree of humility. Therefore, as the merit of inferiors is increased both by the perfections and imperfections of their superiors, so the merit of superiors increases by the perfections and imperfections of inferiors."[40]

Jesus could have added, "It will be a win-win situation all around."

What do you think?

# 39

# Dear Diary

Have you ever kept a diary? Going back over your entries after many years can stir up all kinds of reactions: sometimes a little disappointment or heartache, sometimes amazement and laughter. What about diaries kept by the saints (of course, at this point we can't rule out that ours might have been kept by a saint, too)?

Blessed James Alberione (1884–1971), founder of the Pauline Family, left us a wonderful little diary from his eighteenth year. The diary has the intriguing name, *"Homo . . . Multis Repletur Miseriis"* (Job 14:1), that translates*"Man . . . Is Full of Trouble,"* and it reads more as a book of good advice. Here are a couple of the gems contained in these pages:

> "For man to attain a good, it is necessary for him to consider what he actually is not. . . ."[41]

> "The careless man cannot be tranquil and orderly, nor correct his defects. While he is not bad, neither is he good."[42]

> "Do not stop when you believe you already love Christ,

because this is not making progress; it is not strength of mind or of will, nor is it proper to a strong spirit."[43]

These are the maxims of a young man who wants holiness, but who recognizes the pursuit of it travels right through his own humanity. There is no other way to being a saint than through one's own spirit. So self-knowledge and self-discipline are essential ingredients. Alberione continues:

"Therefore, I want to imitate the example of that friend of mine [a fellow seminarian who died)]. What fortitude in suffering! So much love amid pains. How much humility in his actions. How much courtesy in his dealings. What prudence in his actions, and in speaking. What wisdom in judging. And did he have many talents? No, it was application in thinking. Did he have natural goodness? The fervent, extreme, tenacious, almost desperate battles he suffered are infinite. All flowed from his genuineness, his power of love.[44]

What we have is not a complete diary. It seems that several portions have been lost. What we do have of Alberione's diary concludes with good advice for spiritual advancement:

Great merits do not lie in doing great things, but in doing diligently and well the little things, too—all that which we have to do. Let us employ the time needed for every action, we will carry it out well, we will please God and our heart.[45]

Can you trace even a little progress in virtue since your youth? How has your life been enriched by this effort?

# 40

# "Since Thou Dost Love"

George Herbert (1593–1633), an Anglo-Welsh poet and Anglican priest, wrote a wonderful little poem entitled "Bittersweet" that opens with this charming line: "Ah, my deare angrie Lord."

But let me quote the poem in its entirety:

Ah, my deare angrie Lord,
Since thou dost love, yet strike,
Cast down, yet help afford;
Sure I will do the like.

I will complain, yet praise,
I will bewail, approve;
And all my sowre-sweet dayes
I will lament, and love.[46]

Daphrose Mukansanga Rugamba (1944–1994), had she known of this poem, could have prayed it daily, because her life had become a daily martyrdom. Her arranged marriage to Cyprien Rugamba (1935–1994), a well-known poet, musician, and choreographer, was very difficult. He had lost his faith after encountering scandals while in the seminary. Later his fiancé, Xaverina, was murdered. In his desire to honor his commitment to her family, he married her cousin, Daphrose. Their marriage was very fruitful, and they had ten children, but Cyprien was unfaithful to Daphrose and neglected his family.

He allowed Daphrose to raise the children as Catholics, but he had no patience with religion. Once in her presence he took a crucifix off the wall and smashed it. Eventually they separated.

In 1982 Cyprien was struck by a rapid paralyzing illness. He felt inspired to write a song about his coming death. The song became an intense spiritual experience leading him back to belief in God. Husband and wife reconciled; Cyprien apologized to Daphrose for his years of cruelty and thanked her for her faithful love.

Although Daphrose had many reasons to complain and be an angry person, she learned to convert her negative impulses into virtue. Her husband, Cyprien, could also have continued on without a thought for his God or his wife, but God offered grace, and they both decided to become more godly, to become collaborators with God's goodness. They opened a center to care for street children and began the Emmanuel Community in Rwanda. Cyprien also tried to end the ethnic tensions threatening the society. He made an impassioned radio appeal that made him a marked man. A death squad invaded their home on April 7, 1994, and assassinated the couple along with six of their children.

Let's pray for couples we know who are experiencing difficulties in their relationships. May they realize that the energy of anger and complaint can be converted into respect, love, and service.

## PART III

# Complaints
# from the Holy Book

# 41

# Red Flags

A famous rabbi was once asked why the Bible tells us about the sins of good men.

The rabbi responded that if it didn't teach us about their wrongdoing, we might not believe in their virtue either.

On the other hand, while authors of saints' biographies in the past tended to edit out anything of the human struggle, the Old Testament stories are unedited. We are allowed in to see the whole story with all the rough edges and sins of the subjects. We can easily relate to these portraits because the Author, God who inspired them, wants us to be encouraged by witnessing their very human efforts, not just his divine intervention. And almost as a proof of this theory, we find complaints woven throughout the stories.

We look at the account of Jacob, the last of the Patriarchs, and his two wives, the sisters Leah and Rachel. Although he only intended to marry Rachel, Jacob was tricked into taking Leah first. When he realized his bride was the wrong sister, he vehemently complained to her father: "What is this that you have done to me? Did I not serve with you for Rachel? Why then have you deceived me?" (Gen 29:25 NRSV). Jacob literally had to work for their father an additional seven years for Rachel.

There was constant rivalry between the two wives, who were both jealous of Jacob's attention. When Leah's son Reuben found some fruit of the special mandrake plant, both women wanted it. To Rachel's plea, Leah lamented: "Is it a small matter that you have taken away my husband? Would you take away my son's mandrakes also?" (Gen 30:15 NRSV). And so it went —back and forth.

In the story of Abraham and Sarah, we find Sarah unloading her grief at not having a child, and more painful yet, enduring the reproach of her maid. Sarah complains to her husband: "May the wrong done to me be on you! I gave my slave girl to your embrace, and when she saw that she had conceived, she looked on me with contempt. May the Lord judge between you and me!" (Gen 16:5 NRSV).

This behavior doesn't shock us because it is so familiar. How often do we find ourselves either prefacing or following up our more egregious wrongs with complaints? They are like an editor's red flags in a manuscript indicating that some mistake has been found.

What might be the larger matters that the complaints in the pages of your life are pointing out?

# 42

# Too Heavy for Me

Among the more dramatic Bible stories is that of Moses who is immediately identified with the Ten Commandments. He was born when the Egyptians had imposed a ban on male births, so Moses was hidden in a basket and placed in the river among the reeds. His discovery by an Egyptian princess saved his life and put into motion the great drama of the liberation of the Chosen People from Egypt. God sent Moses to the Pharaoh to demand the people's freedom. He was, of course, refused because the Egyptians relied on the enforced labor of the Jews. God intervened with a series of miraculous signs, including plagues of locusts and frogs, culminating with the death of all firstborn sons. Pharaoh relented and let the people go to the desert for a religious celebration. When Pharaoh realized they had no intention of returning, he sent his troops after them. This led quickly to the miraculous escape route created by the parting of the Red Sea.

When Moses was invited to a conversation with God on Mount Sinai, God gave the stone tablets of the Law. While Moses was with God, the people grew impatient and made a golden calf to worship. This lack of faith gained the people forty years of wandering in the desert. I suggest you reread the whole story that runs from Exodus through Deuteronomy to grasp the impact of God's interaction with this people he had chosen as his own, to whom he was entrusting his whole plan of salvation.

Despite the full weight of this unique relationship, we see the people are no different from ourselves: they are weak, distracted, often fickle, discontent, and demanding. What happens? This very sacred portion of history becomes a complaining match just as it would have been if we were there. The people complain about the conditions in general: *"Why did you lead us out here to die?"* Nothing satisfies them and they eventually hand a shopping list to Moses: *"This is what we are missing in this wilderness."* Moses turns on God: "I am not able to carry all these people alone, for they are too heavy for me. If this is the way you are going to treat me, put me to death at once . . ." (Num 11:14–15 NRSV).

When Moses begged God to release him from the burden of carrying all the people (that is, their infidelity) on his own shoulders, it reminded me of Jesus' cry to the Father in Gethsemane to take the impending cross from his shoulders. How often has some suffering we complain about and pray to have taken away been of indispensable help to someone else? Does a specific example come to mind?

# 43

# Complaining Prophet

Of all the challenging messages of God's prophets in the Old Testament, the most relatable for us is from Jonah (see Jon 1–4).

First, Jonah didn't want the job of prophesying to the totally sinful city of Nineveh. In fact, he ran (or rather sailed) away from it.

God kept Jonah in his sight, however, and sent a big storm that petrified the sailors. They tried to rouse Jonah from sleep to pray for deliverance. When that didn't work, they cast lots to see whose fault it was that they were in such danger. Jonah was the unlucky winner and so he was tossed into the sea in the hope of calming God's anger. A large fish, often identified as a whale, swallowed Jonah who immediately recognized his next best move was to pray.

God gave Jonah a second chance, *and* a second call to prophesy. So, as he was drying out, Jonah went to the vast city of Nineveh. Traveling from one end to the other, his message was simple: "Repent. Forty days left before destruction!" The whole population embraced his message, and from the king to the lowly animals, all put on sackcloth and sat in ashes. God was pleased and decided not to punish them for their sins.

What an unpleasant surprise for Jonah, however, who was hoping against hope that they wouldn't repent. He was furious and complained furiously: "Isn't this what I predicted, Lord? That's exactly why I fled in the beginning. You are too kind and merciful, too slow to anger and way too forgiving. So, now, just kill me. I'd rather die than live!" Jonah turned on his heel and climbed a hill to camp out and wait for whatever would happen.

Employing his patience and kindness, God made a shady plant grow up over Jonah, which pleased him. But next day God sent a worm to take out the plant. Then when the sun rose, Jonah prayed for death again. God asked, "Is it right for you to be angry about the plant?" "Yes," retorted Jonah, "Enough to die!"

"Do you think it's okay for you to be upset over something you didn't plant or cause to grow?" God asked. "So, then what about my concern for Nineveh where there are a hundred and twenty thousand people who don't know their right hand from their left, not to mention the animals?"

This is one of those famous open-ended stories. What do you imagine God wants us to conclude from his Jonah tale?

# 44

# Where Were You?

How many stories can be told about kitchen complaints? We have many here in the convent, and I'm sure every family has some too. In the Gospel, of course, the best teachable moment kitchen complaint comes straight from the lips of Saint Martha.

The story unfolds in Luke 10:38–42 with "a woman named Martha receiving Jesus into her home." So right away we know that Martha is not simply the kitchen maid. She is actually the lady of the house who has a sister named Mary and a brother Lazarus who stays quietly in the background. We don't know if they've met Jesus before, but as soon as he is inside and talking, Mary settles herself at his feet. After a while Martha comes to complain, and in order to get the necessary result, she addresses her complaint to Jesus even though it is meant for Mary. "Lord, doesn't it matter to you that my sister has left me alone? Tell her to give me a hand!" (It sounds like she is overwhelmed. Perhaps the Twelve came along with Jesus.)

Did Jesus quickly shoo Mary into the kitchen? No, he gently chided Martha for being so anxious and upset "about many things." "Mary has chosen the better part, which will not be taken from her." He didn't say Martha's part was not important (after all, there would be no meal without her efforts). Perhaps he is thinking of how Mary will anoint him later in the Gospel (see Jn 12:3), but more likely it is just recognition that each person has a part to play in the stories of life. Some parts are better, while others are necessary. Before we judge, let's think again about the comparison made by Saint Thérèse's sister Pauline about the glass and thimble: which is fuller?

Some time after this dinner Jesus hears that Lazarus is deathly ill. His sisters are summoning Jesus, but he puts the trip off. When he does arrive several days later, Jesus is met by Martha who greets him with the complaint, "If you had come when we called you, Lazarus wouldn't have died, but I still trust you will receive whatever you ask in prayer." Martha offers an amazing act of faith in the final resurrection and in Jesus as Messiah. Mary follows and almost repeats again Martha's anxiety, but dissolves in tears. Jesus responds to both of them by raising Lazarus.

Think of a time when you complained and try to remember what prompted the complaint, but more importantly, what you hoped your complaint would accomplish.

# 45

# Complaint Inside a Complaint

A curious set of complaints occurs within the prelude to the Passover account in John's Gospel (12:1–11). The scene is a banquet given in Jesus' honor at the home of Mary, Martha, and the newly raised Lazarus. It should be noted that this same incident is told in Matthew 26:6–13 and Mark 14:3–9 with slightly different characters. To be fair, in John's account there is no specific mention of whose house this was. The other accounts say it was the house of Simon the leper. In any case, the essential element is this: a woman (here, Mary of Bethany) anoints Jesus with a pound of very expensive oil, an act that fills the house with perfume *and* complaints. The first complaint is voiced by Judas Iscariot: "What a waste! Why wasn't this oil sold for three hundred days' wages and the money given to the poor?" The second complaint comes as an editorial note by the author of this Gospel who states that Judas wasn't concerned for the poor but for the purse. He kept the money and would help himself to the contents. This is a duly noted historical complaint.

Jesus defends Mary for her prophetic foresight. Her anointing would be for his burial. Judas was reprimanded: "The poor you profess to care for are always around; I instead will not be."

It seems that Judas fell victim to his own faults. We can't be sure what came first, but three things are obvious in these few verses of Scripture. Judas was a thief; he was a complainer; and he was a traitor (from this banquet he goes to the chief priests to turn Jesus in). Scripture tells us that "out of the heart the mouth speaks." So, the heart of the matter for Judas wasn't that the poor would be deprived but that he would have access to less. It is possible that he expected the oil simply to be given as a gift to Jesus who would hand it to Judas to sell for them. Either way, his heart wasn't as attuned to Jesus as Mary's was. She did what her spirit prompted (remember, they both witnessed the miraculous rising of Lazarus not that long before), whereas Judas only saw a new opportunity that would benefit himself.

You and I need to study our own complaints carefully to see what is at the heart of them.

# 46

# Two Men Walk Into . . .

We are familiar with some of the many "two men walked into a bar" jokes. They generally begin by saying: "Once there was a priest . . . and a rabbi" or "a politician and a plumber." Jesus uses the same literary device to set up his essay on complaining: *"Two men went up into the Temple to pray, one a Pharisee and the other a tax collector"* (see Lk 18:9–14).

The picture that Jesus paints here is of two men auspiciously in the same place at the same time for the same purpose. One lives out the Law as perfectly as humanly possible. He is a Pharisee, after all, and that means he has spent years in intense study. His life is dedicated to observing the letter of that Law. He takes a prayerful position up front as is expected of such an exemplar of observance. The other man, hoping to attract no attention except from the One who truly matters, cramps himself up in a darkened back corner not even raising his head. Both men began their prayers sincerely enough. The first one recited for God all the ways he was observant; the second, keeping his head bowed, kept beating his breast repeating: "O God, forgive me, a sinner!" Okay so far, but then Jesus points out that the Pharisee inserted comparisons and a blaring complaint about the tax collector: "O God, I give You thanks because I'm not like other men, greedy, unjust, adulterers—or even like this tax collector."

The tax collecting profession was not well respected as it can be today. It was, first of all, carried out for the Roman occupiers and so the tax collector was a civil servant of an alien government. Second, tax collectors were allowed to add to the required tax in order to support themselves, so often they were perceived as dishonest men. The Pharisee's words make a big dent in the beautiful prayer experience he has been involved in. Jesus lauds the humility and truthfulness of the tax collector and says, "He went down to his house pardoned and reconciled with God rather than the other one, because: "Everyone who exalts himself will be humbled, while whoever humbles himself will be exalted."

Are you ever tempted to make comparisons with others in church? Do you hear yourself thinking how well-behaved your children are and how irritating those other children are; how much more generous you are with time and talent than others?

# 47

# Front for Faults

Sometimes we use complaints as a front for our faults, as a cover or an excuse.

One day a little boy brought home a report card that had fine, passing grades for every subject except for conduct. His parents asked for the reason and their son simply answered, "Well, Mom and Dad, the thing is, conduct is my most difficult subject."

Another more familiar example of using complaints to cover for our defects appears in the Gospel of Matthew 18:21–35 in the parable of the unforgiving servant. The story goes that a man was called in to pay a considerable debt he had amassed (not unlike folks today with large credit card debts). "If you can't settle this right now, I'm going to have to call the police," the lender declared. The man, plus his wife and children, would go to prison, and all his property would be sold to accommodate the debt. Well, it appears the man created quite a scene. He fell down crying and pleading, "Be patient with me and I'll pay back everything." This won the day, and he was absolved of the debt.

We are shocked by what follows! This newly forgiven debtor turns on a fellow debtor, unreasonably demanding payment of a much smaller debt. We are told that he went out and *found* someone who owed him money. He didn't just come upon a fellow debtor, but went out looking for someone who owed him. This is what often happens as a cause to complain. A person has a self-perceived reason to go on a rant, but turns the rant on the activity or motivation of someone else. Whatever real, or imagined, affront the person comes after, it is made to carry the guilt and humiliation of the original confrontation.

This method of covering up for one's mistakes may seem clever, or at least expedient, to the doer, but a person's character is more easily discerned from outside observation than from one's own inner cunning. Here is a little example: a certain man spoke openly of the failings of another in the presence of a very wise man. When he had finished, the wise man said, "Thank you for exposing all your failings to me as you glibly rattled off the failings of your friend."

Isn't it true that what we accuse another of, whether rightly or wrongly, is very similar to our own faults?

# 48

# Trashing

When I was young, I did something pretty strange, even by my standards. One evening after supper, I postponed my particular chore—emptying the trash—to watch a television show. Whatever the show was, I fell asleep. My mom finally roused me, but I wasn't fully awake. She said something about going to do my chore and then going on to bed. But I did wake up with a start at my mother's command, "Stop that right now! What are you doing?" I pried open my eyes and found, to my horror, that I had emptied a little of the trash into each of the cereal bowls that were set up for breakfast. Needless to say, I was sent up to bed promptly while my mother and sister cleaned up my "dream" job.

I was reminded of this bit of my history when reading one of the conferences of our foundress, Mother Thecla Merlo. She exhorted us "to pass over many little things, without criticizing and without telling it to everyone. When one sweeps, she doesn't put dirt on the table, but gets rid of it where no one sees it. Let us know how to be compassionate, how to hide the defects of others."[47]

Although I had unintentionally put dirt on the table, I'm not as diligent about compassion and hiding others' defects as I should be. Why is it so easy to comply unconsciously, without even knowing the command, and yet, more important precepts are so easily overlooked? One would think that compassion and not just excusing, but hiding, the defects of others would be the more natural thing. It seems, however, that the less virtuous response comes more spontaneously to us.

Maybe the less virtuous is more natural. I am thinking of Adam and Eve. In their biography, the Book of Genesis, there's a lot of "he said/she said" dialogue. They were special friends of God (well, probably the only friends of God) in the Garden of Eden. God had given them a lot of latitude, just one thing to avoid—the tree in the middle of the Garden. They failed miserably. When God confronted them, he had to listen to a litany of complaints. Supposedly Adam and Eve were still in love at this time (the incident doesn't seem long after they were literally "made for each other"), but we hear them going at one another.

Blame is definitely a trait inherited from Adam and Eve, and it is an indirect way of complaining. Reflect on a time you blamed another for something that turned out badly. What was the result?

# 49

# More Trashing

The story of our first parents, Adam and Eve, illustrates our problem with complaining. God has now gone to look for them. They did not show up at the appointed time when God came for his daily walk in the Garden. This kind of break in the schedule is never a good sign. God finds them hiding among the plants. "Why are you hiding?" he asks. "Uh, well, because we're naked," they reply. *They're hiding and they recognize they are naked;* God realizes that someone else has been there. Adam and Eve have been listening to someone other than God. "So," God said, "you have eaten of the tree that was off limits!" Adam points to Eve and complains. "The woman you gave me handed the fruit to me to eat. And so, naturally, I ate it." Now it was her turn, and God asked Eve, "What exactly did you do?" Eve pointed out the snake and complained, "The serpent tricked me, and I ate the fruit."

So much for compassion—suffering together. They turned on each other; they didn't hide the other's fault. Instead they complained—lamenting each other. They threw each other under the bus, so to speak. This is what complaining does, and we should note who promoted the whole incident: the devil posing as a snake.

Neither Adam nor Eve asked for forgiveness. Presumably this oversight was due to their being the first two humans and having lived a faultless life up until this moment. They had never experienced the need to apologize: neither the why nor the how. The problem is that they set a precedent for us who now find it difficult and painful to humiliate ourselves before God for our transgressions.

God then taught them compassion by sending them out of the Garden to face difficulty and suffering together. And now, as God points out, they do know good and evil—by experience.

When forced to reflect on them or endure their consequences, we do learn from our complaints. Think of an occasion when you learned a valuable lesson from a complaint.

# 50

# In the Beginning

Was this the origin of complaining? Did this tendency actually start with Adam and Eve? Is it part of the basic human self-defense mechanism? The first sin seems to have been disobedience stemming from pride, addressed with complaint.

When theologians and Scripture scholars think about our beginnings, they speak of the first humans as being pure images of their Creator. We have difficulty seriously imagining what this better version was like because all we know is the flawed version. All the way back through human history right to the Garden, and all the way forward to our very selves we see nothing but struggle. Fortunately for us, our time is permeated with the redeeming presence of Christ. His coming into the human family has rejuvenated us by removing sin and filling in all those flaws with his grace.

The one big inheritance we all received from our once-perfect first parents, however, is their first sin, the original sin, which is also our first sin. Thanks to the mercy of God, this original sin is removed with the sacrament of Baptism, but the debilitating flaws still remain with us. Blessed James Alberione points out, "Each one comes to Christ with one great problem—*himself.* This problem, ever more urgent and inescapable, is to take the right 'road,' to set oneself exactly in the 'truth,' in view of a sure and full development of 'life.'"[48]

Alberione's advice is to take ourselves entirely in hand, that is, our whole self, mind, will, and heart and set out to follow Jesus, who introduces himself as "Way, Truth, and Life." It is the grandest of projects and the simplest of projects. So how should we attack this venture?

One of Blessed Alberione's earliest pupils, now the Venerable Maggiorino Vigolungo (1904–1918), was a youngster from the Piedmont region of Italy, with a difficult name and an ingenious plan "to be a tad better every day." He did not resolve to implement the entire realm of asceticism overnight, to wake up each morning to the perfection of Christ, or to throw himself into the path of every heretic and enemy of the Church. No, but he could be a little better each day. So can we.

How do I address each new day: as a problem to complain about or as an opportunity to be a better follower of Christ? What area of your life are you trying to improve?

PART IV

# Learning from the Saints How to Handle Complaining

# 51

# Look the Part

Now we aren't getting off scot-free. If we learn from those who were holy before us, then we need to offer this same example to those whose paths we cross, as well as to those who will follow us.

Every once in a while, someone will come up to me and say, "You look so upset. What is the matter?" My responses vary, but my favorite is to say, "Nothing's wrong. I'm just trying to make this the new normal."

Occasionally, I also hear, "Smile, Sister. It doesn't cost any more." My standard comeback for this one is, "Sorry, but my smile was installed upside down."

There is also what I consider an old wives' tale that claims it takes more muscles to frown than to smile. My reply is, "Humbug! I don't need to exert any effort at all to frown. I'm just doing what comes naturally!"

In fact, I used to think my face was pleasant at rest, but I fear it isn't. Rather, it makes me appear unpleasant or displeased all the time, in fact, perpetually crabby. So how do we maintain the illusion of being a happy Christian 24/7?

For some the answer is simply to keep up appearances by smiling and looking like a happy Christian should. Of course, we really are happy, joyful, content people, thanks to our Baptism into Christ. *We are Alleluia people!* Amen to that! That's not fiction, but fact. We are, however, at the same time children of men (and women). And we are subject to all the natural afflictions of the human family. We are victims of bad attitudes, bad hair days, bum legs, bum deals, hot flashes, and burnout, just to mention a few human happenings that can give our *Alleluia* a run for its money. Do these failures cancel out our Christian joy? No, they place it in the midst of reality —where human life journeys to the kingdom.

Jesus Christ does not work from the outside in, but vice versa, from the inside out. He never promised to perfect the details of our existence, or to reestablish us in the state of soul before the fall of Adam and Eve. He *did* promise that he and his Father would come and make their abode within us, and that his Spirit would be with us to guide, strengthen, and inspire us *until we breathe forth our soul in peace with him.*

We pray: "Dear Lord, help me face the challenges of my daily walk. I want to stay in your company. Let me wear my faith well. Amen."

Yet, we still complain. What does this inclination tell you about how gentle and patient God is with us?

# 52

# My Sainted "Other"

Often we hear someone refer to his or her long-suffering mother as a saint. She was pious and motherly, a moral compass, and an unwavering comfort. Perhaps she prayed so frequently that she could be thought of as a living rosary. Many look back on their mom with this type of reverence. She is/was a sainted individual.

As I embark on the discovery of my own deeper life, I can see at least a dim reflection of my mother in me. Will I ever become more than her "mini-me"? Can I ever be judged as "holy"? Honestly, it is a hard sell right now. My faults and failings are many. Of the two angelic beings seated on my shoulders, the little left-leaning red one seems to have the upper hand. You're being too hard on yourself, it subtly whispers. That is probably true, but I fear I am more lulled by the little red guy than startled by the white-winged one who stresses the importance of vigilance.

Oh, the human condition! It seems we can't live with it, and we can't live without it. If I sit still for a moment, however, and consider what I have been given by way of grace and favor from

God—you know, all the sacraments, all the blessings, and prayers, particularly those of my mother (and father)—I should be fully committed to the program of holiness. I need to always consider *my own sainted "other"*—the saint I am meant to become. I need to remain open and available to God.

Whether we like it or not, we must be resigned to the fact that unless we commit some deliberate serious offense toward God (a mortal sin), we *are* saints, which is how the early Church describes us. One of the earliest descriptions of the followers of Jesus was this: they are saints. "To all those in Rome who are beloved of God and are called to be saints, grace and peace be with you from God our Father and the Lord Jesus Christ" (Rm 1:7 TNT; see also 1 Cor 1:2; Eph 1:1).

Here is a challenge for all of us who spend time lamenting the qualities we don't possess: list your characteristics—good, better, and best. Which ones might have come from your parents?

# 53

# Statuesque

Let me tell you about my "one and done" foray into statuary. You've heard of people accused of posing for animal crackers. Usually they're doing outlandish things for attention. Well, once I was in charge of playing reel-to-reel taped meditations by our founder over the amplifier in chapel. I would peer out from the sacristy to get someone's attention and assure myself that everyone could hear.

All the sisters were so recollected that I couldn't get anyone's attention. Every time I did this, I had the temptation to bring a vase of flowers and a lit candle with me. I'd place these in front of myself as I piously posed on a little stepstool on one side of the sanctuary. How long would I be there before someone would notice? What kind of reaction would I get? "I hadn't even heard that she died, never mind a statue already!" Or "What audacity and in the sanctuary at that!" I would have been happy with a little muffled laugh or cough.

What would my statue look like?

Oh, the Church would never make a statue of me the way I actually look! No, no—frayed habit, tilting glasses, shoes scuffed and worn—not to mention bad posture (in all of her corrections my mother never mentioned how bad my posture would look on a statue). Ah, but bless those statue makers! They always gloss things over. In Rome I went into a statuary shop that had a row of identical male saints and a row of identical female saints on display. All that distinguished them were the articles they held or the color of what they were wearing. Of course, most of those saints were never photographed or even painted in their lifetime so we will never know how they looked.

Allow a small digression here. Notice that I said these lines of wooden saints were distinguishable only by the color of what they wore: all in habits or vestments—that is a call to many of you, dear readers. We, the Church, need more lay saints. Religious orders and dioceses promote the causes of religious, priests, and bishops; lay folk are largely overlooked. And this, even though as adults most of us look fondly and reverently at our mothers and grandmothers as saints. (Our fathers and grandfathers as well.)

Note well: The call to universal holiness is not just for Catholics and Christians, but it is a universal call.

When you become a saint, what will distinguish or decorate your statue?

# 54

# Truth Be Told

The topic comes up now and then of the Chapter of Faults, a custom of many religious communities, mostly in the past. I wonder what pops into the minds of those outside religious life when they hear of this. It's a mysterious term at best. Normally we think of chapters as divisions within a book or as the title of a local branch of a widespread organization, for example, the local chapter of the Optimist Club. What is a Chapter of Faults? It might be understood as a type of recovery meeting, as those held for any form of addictive behavior, where literally the members of the Chapter of Faults gather to accuse themselves or to be accused of their faults, usually minor infractions of the common rule. It is a way of humbling oneself in the hope of doing better.

Complaining is a classic example of a fault to accuse yourself of or be accused of by the others. Complaints are one of the biggest disrupters of our life together. Families know this all too well. In fact, family meals often turn into a kind of domestic chapter of faults. Parents may need to give some urgent advice, or they may have a correction for one child that the others also need to hear. In this setting, things that might lead to complaining can be aired out. Even more importantly, all those involved have the opportunity to know one another better, in a more intimate light, thereby stemming the urge to complain against one another later.

When I was a newly professed sister, I lived with another slightly older sister, who was light years ahead in common sense. One day she quietly approached me and said, "Sister, may I say something to you?" I don't recall what she wanted to say (although it might have been about complaining), but I have always cherished her considerate method.

So, whether we are able to self-correct or whether we need correction from others, the habit of complaining requires attention. It is very Christian to counsel one another. *The Didache*, one of the earliest Christian instruction manuals, had this to say:

> Avoid being a grumbler, opinionated, or evil-minded. These will lead next to blasphemy. Instead be gentle-hearted and *you will inherit the earth*. Be patient and merciful, innocent, subdued, and good. Hold with caution, as most precious, every instruction that has been passed on to you.[49]

Are you able to offer advice or correction with gentleness and respect? Can you explain how grumbling could lead to blasphemy?

# 55

# Wishing Well

"I really do feel bad for those people. Look at them begging from drivers at the intersection. But, actually, they should be working. If they can stand there all day, they could be holding down a job. It's kind of pitiful, you know."

Has that ever been you complaining about the people cluttering our street corners or, for that matter, clambering at our borders? If so, what exactly is the problem? If it's that they are an eyesore to our otherwise perfect lives, you haven't looked around much. You haven't seen the *unseen* eyesores of our society. If you feel they are taking advantage of the goodness of others (yourself included), it is because you *have* an advantage. If you are perturbed because someone should be doing something about this situation, remember that *you are someone.*

Dorothy Day (1897–1980) would know how to answer those questions for us. She was a very modern, yet very traditional saintly woman (although she shuddered at the thought of being considered "saint"-worthy). Along with Peter Maurin, she founded the Catholic Worker Movement.

Dorothy championed not only the rights of the poor but our right to serve the poor.

> What right has any one of us to security when God's poor are suffering? What right have I to sleep in a comfortable bed when so many are sleeping in the shadows of buildings here in this neighborhood of the Catholic Worker office? What right have we to food when many are hungry, or to liberty when . . . so many . . . are in jail?
>
> To those in whose minds these questions are stirring, these words are directed:
>
> "Today if you shall hear My voice, harden not your hearts."[50]

In 1964 Dorothy wrote: "The more you give away, the more the Lord will give you to give away. It is a growth in faith. It is the attitude of the man whose life of common sense and faith is integrated."[51]

If a brother or sister needs clothes and lacks food for the day and one of you says to them, "Go in peace; stay warm and eat well!" what good is it? And so, faith by itself is dead, unless it is manifested in works (see Jas 2:16).

Dorothy would remind us that the Gospel cancels forever our right to discriminate between the poor who are deserving and those who are undeserving. What does this say to your heart?

Another scary thought: "For the mouth speaks from the abundance of the heart" (Mt 12:34 TNT). What do my complaints say of my heart?

# 56

# Terrible News

One of the most depressing things we do each day is tune into the news. Some broadcasts purposefully include an upbeat story simply to offer some relief from the barrage of bad news they are required to report.

Nevertheless, we can't help but be upset and annoyed by the general negativity we are exposed to during these programs. And the graphic images accompanying the reporting only make matters worse.

Because we refer to the Gospel as the Good News, we often ask one another: "Are you going to watch the *bad* news tonight?" Almost every night one of us will let out an exasperated sigh and declare: "Can this get any worse? What's wrong with people these days?" Others won't even tune in to the news: "I am boycotting it until they get their act together."

God has blessed us with free will, however, so whatever happens in the world is up to us (the whole human race that is). We can content ourselves with just ranting at the screen and complaining to one another, but that isn't very productive, and hardly a Christian response. Jesus himself assures us that he was born because "God *so loved* the world . . ." (Jn 3:16 NRSV). So, what then?

We could take our cue from a very unlikely person, Servant of God Mother Scholastica Rivata (1897–1987), first superior general of the Pious Disciples of the Divine Master. The mission of her congregation springs from the love of Jesus living in the Eucharist, in the priesthood, and in the liturgy. The Disciples have a more contemplative vocation than most other active religious, but Mother Scholastica's advice to her sisters was this: "Read the newspapers, listen to the radio and television in order to be aware of the needs of souls and to pray for all the needs of the country, of the Church, of the souls of all humanity."[52]

Some folks might still object that this advice would be a distraction to prayer, but not so according to Mother Scholastica who went so far as to bring the newspaper with her to adoration. Her intention of glorifying God and bringing peace to humanity necessitated praying over the events of the day and for all those affected by them.

You may want to find ways that you can pray the news in order to bring all the events of our history to God's throne, to thank him for his blessings and to beg his mercy.

# 57

# Imperfect Perfection

We all have our moments of enlightenment—those perfect days. Then there was the day I cheerfully announced: "You know, Sister, I would be a saint if it weren't for a few major defects."

I started reading C. S. Lewis' masterpiece, *Mere Christianity*, and was immediately struck by his thoughts on human nature. In the first chapter he writes:

> I am not preaching, and Heaven knows I do not pretend to be better than anyone else. I am only trying to call attention to a fact; the fact that this year, or this month, or, more likely, this very day, we have failed to practice ourselves the kind of behaviour we expect from other people. There may be all sorts of excuses for us.[53]

Excuses aside, we voice our expectations all too often as complaints. "Why did you do it this way when you knew it should be done that way?" As if we had the secret code for perfect conduct!

This kind of perfection in our human conduct, in our manner of doing things, is only surface perfection, and it means nothing in relation to the perfection of holiness.

If Christ hadn't said to his disciples, "So you be perfect as your Heavenly Father is perfect" (Mt 5:48 TNT), would we be as consumed as we are by the prospect of imperfection? I would say, yes, we would be because, although those words of Christ are high-end motivation, in our personal search for spiritual perfection we are subject to the original sin of pride. Pride places us in a state of perpetual perfectionism.

Our perfection, however, is not going to happen until the last trumpet summons us to the universal judgment. Why will it take so long? It's because there is no perfection except as a reflection of God who is perfect. We strive for perfection because we are drawn to Divine perfection. We find all that is good, beautiful, and true about ourselves as a small reflection of the eternal Truth, Goodness, and Beauty that we know as God. And part of our striving is simply to hold on to what we have of God's perfection.

Perfection isn't holiness; perfection is the hoped-for result, but holiness is the journey to perfection. Perhaps you have mastered the Lord's Prayer in another language, but where is holiness in this? You can recite the words perfectly, but have you said the prayer holily?

# 58

# Perfect Imperfection

Where do you suppose this chapter is going? We just finished talking about how our perfection is imperfect, and now we want to look at the perfection of imperfection? At least we feel like we're on a first-name basis with imperfection, whereas we are still only admiring perfection from afar.

In our congregation we have a prayer we call the *Secret of Success* in which we acknowledge that we are weak, ignorant, incapable, and wanting in all respects. All too true, right? Perfect!

Christian perfection is integration of life, getting every aspect of our life in order. In this way we are better prepared to love God fully and to love our neighbors truly. Saint Paul teaches: "Above all, clothe yourselves with love, which binds everything together in perfect harmony" (Col 3:14 NRSV).

This perfection is, rather, *perfectibility*, which means progressively realizing the divine ideal who is Jesus Christ, the highest and most complete fulfillment of the human person. We must learn to rely entirely on Jesus.

How best to do this? Take some advice from Dom John Chapman, OSB:

We used to think we were good—now we know we are not. We suffer from this, and, as we realize our imperfections more and more, we seem to be going backwards. Only we have got to be *resigned* to seeing these imperfections. We must not make light of them, in the sense of not hating them; but it is quite good to laugh at them. The more we ridicule ourselves the better, as we see our constant failures.

So it is better to make *"acts of humility"*: 1) either *laughing* at ourselves, for our failures, carelessness, want of love and so forth; or 2) say, "You see, O Lord, how silly I am—this is all you can expect!"; or 3) "I am delighted to see how imperfect I am—reveal more to me of my wretchedness."

We say, of course: "You see what I am, without your grace." Only don't think God is not giving you a great deal of grace. It is an enormous grace to be left to be conscious of our own want of recollection and of energy."[54]

Take a little prayer time to reflect with Saint Thérèse. What is the happiness she refers to in these words?

"How happy I am to see myself imperfect and be in need of God's mercy."[55]

# 59

# Facial Recognition

"Anyone who is a hearer of the word and not a doer is like a man observing his own face in a mirror, for he looks at himself, then turns away and at once forgets what he looked like" (Jas 1:23–24 TNT). This person is unable to act on his identity. He hears God's Word, but can't see how it is lived.

On the natural level each of us has a mental image of our self—not necessarily of our physical appearance, but of our *presence*, of how we present ourselves to the world. This image can be shaken or shattered by a negative comment or criticism. *"That's not me. That's crazy,"* we mutter. But, if we are honest and reflective, what was said will strike a chord. Even if it isn't true, a little reflection will help us see what there is about us that prompted the comment.

Ultimately, this cherished *look* of ours is the reflection of God we carry about within us. We should be convinced that our mirror image is found in the faces of our neighbors also.

The book of early Franciscan stories, *The Little Flowers of St. Francis,* recounts a story about Saint Louis, King of France. While on a pilgrimage he alters his route to seek out Brother

Giles in Perugia. Louis and Giles said nothing to each other, but merely embraced and piously knelt in each other's presence. After quite a while in this silence, they both rose and went their separate ways. The brothers who witnessed their meeting thought it was a wasted opportunity for the two saints. It upset them so much that they complained to Brother Giles: "How is it possible that you never spoke a word to the king who came so far just to see you? Was there no advice you could have given him?"

Patiently Giles explained that there was no need for words because they mutually understood the other's desires as they looked into each other's heart. "Words would only have confused the mysterious conversation God placed in our hearts. Fear not, the king left greatly consoled."[56]

How often have you acted out what you have heard in the Gospel? Do you feel yourself "on the same page" with other Christians?

# 60

# Life Vision

When a couple marries, they have a vision of their life together, or at least what they hope life will bring. A major component of their hopes concerns children: when will they come, how many will they be, and will they be healthy. The marriage in 2008 of Chiara Corbella (1984–2012) and Enrico Petrillo was no different. They did not have long to wait for their first pregnancy. In 2009 they were anxiously awaiting their first child, but an ultrasound revealed the little girl was anencephalic and could not survive. An abortion was advised, but both parents were adamantly opposed. They would bring her to birth and accompany her to heaven. Maria Grazia lived for forty minutes, was baptized, and died. When people lauded the parents' beautiful attitude toward life, Chiara stated simply: "We do not at all feel courageous because in reality the only thing that we have done is said yes, one step at a time."

News of their second pregnancy several months later also brought them up short when the ultrasound showed a son severely disabled. He had no legs, and his lower organs were malformed. Again, Chiara and Enrico refused to consider terminating the pregnancy; however, Chiara fought long and hard with God internally. She strongly disputed with him but accepted God's will with serenity. Little Davide following his sister was born, baptized, and given back to God.

The third pregnancy began with some trepidation, but much hope in God's provident care. This time the baby was going to be healthy. Soon, however, tragedy struck again; this time it involved Chiara herself. She was diagnosed with cancer on her tongue. The choice was whose life to favor. Abortion wasn't in the equation, but without aggressive steps, the cancer would metastasize. Chiara turned to prayer begging God, "Why don't you help me? I know you can!" With the strong support of Enrico and her family and friends, Chiara was able to carry baby Francesco to term. But her own health deteriorated rapidly.

Some thought her choice was irresponsible, but a priest friend affirmed her saying: "Chiara didn't die because of Francesco, but she gave her life for him." Nearing her end, unable to speak, Chiara consoled everyone with her serenity and her smile.

If we question her decision, the Servant of God Chiara Petrillo might challenge us with words from *The Imitation of Christ* (I, 22):

> Who has everything going the way they want?! Neither you, nor I, nor anyone living on earth. . . . For whom do things go better? No doubt it is the one who is willing to suffer something for God's sake.[57]

# 61

# Two Who Could Have

How often in passing conversation we might ask a friend: "So, how are you doing?" Our friend's reply: "Oh, I can't complain!" "What?" we say, "Don't be silly! Of course, you can complain, you're just not trying!"

Let me tell you about Charlie and Lolo, two men who could have complained but didn't. Charlie was from Puerto Rico and Lolo from Spain. They were contemporaries and are now both titled as blessed. Charlie lived from 1918–1963 and Lolo from 1920–1971. They could have been world-class complainers, but they wouldn't even try. And here's why.

Charlie, whose given name was Carlos Manuel Cecilio Rodriguez Santiago, was a devout, creative, and fun-loving man, in love with the liturgy. He published a liturgical newsletter that he sent without cost to anyone who asked for it. He wanted everyone to share his love for the Easter Vigil liturgy. He had even thought he might become a priest someday. At thirteen, however, after saving an infant cousin from a dog attack, Charlie developed ulcerative colitis, a constant source of suffering. Despite this illness, Charlie was active as a youth minister, catechist, and in hospital ministry until his challenge became a deadly stomach cancer.

Lolo, whose given name was Manuel Lozano Garrido, was a journalist. I can't say he was an aspiring journalist whose career was cut short because his career blossomed and flourished despite progressive paralysis and eventual blindness. Lolo was greatly devoted to the Eucharist. As a youngster during the Spanish Civil War, he concealed the Sacrament and brought it to those in hiding or imprisoned until he was arrested. While in prison, Lolo contracted an illness that pursued him into adulthood and forced him to give up a teaching career. In constant pain, he was confined to a wheelchair and eventually was only able to use one finger to type. When that finger, too, became paralyzed, he dictated to his sister. From his joyous soul, Lolo authored nine books and many articles. He even initiated a prayer network called *Sinai* that consisted of cloistered nuns and disabled persons who would pray and suffer for journalists. In fact, Lolo described his own profession as "disabled." With all of his pain, his immobility, his dependence on others, his blindness, Lolo would never complain. He compared himself to a hydro-electric plant whose secret energy was from prayer and suffering.

How would you explain the extraordinary attitude these two men shared? How do the sacraments and the liturgy influence your life?

# 62

# Alberione's Advice

Here is a very pointed quip from *The Imitation of Christ*: "If you cannot make yourself what you would want to be, why do you have expectations about others?" (I, 16)[58]

It's very important advice for us complainers. First scrutiny should be given to ourselves. The following are thoughts of Blessed James Alberione on self-assessment.

— It's very important that we examine our attitude in our relations with others. The good, mature person who is capable of adapting himself to others is a powerful force, while the contrary is one of the greatest impediments to good. The person of character is he who possesses strong convictions and endeavors firmly and consistently to conform his life to them.

— A pleasant disposition implies the blending of goodness and firmness, of charm and strength, of frankness and tact, thus deserving the love and esteem of those with whom we deal. The ill-natured person, instead, is rude in his manners and allows his egoism to dominate him. He is disagreeable and lacks goodness and delicacy.

— All of us have some sharp angles in our character, some unpleasant traits . . . but we should live like people who love one another. "Love is patient; love is kind" (1 Cor 13:4 NRSV).

— Let us not deceive ourselves. We are not living with perfect people and we are not perfect either. The best among us are those striving for perfection. "Help carry one another's burdens" (see Gal 6:2). However, those who realize that they are a burden should reflect on their serious responsibility before God and should amend their ways.

— Some are able to discover the good all the time! They take note of the smallest favor received and they are quick to forget any wrong done them. . . .

— Those who continually see what is wrong and always have something of which to accuse others or rebuke them are not goodhearted. Sometimes it takes only a smile to settle many things.[59]

How would you explain Saint Paul's injunction:

Complete my joy by being of one mind, sharing the same love, being united in spirit, and thinking as one. Do nothing out of selfishness or desire to boast; instead, in a spirit of humility toward one another, regard others as better than yourselves. Each of you should look out for the rights of others, rather than looking after your own rights. Have the same outlook among you that Christ Jesus had. (Phil 2:2–5 TNT)

# 63

# Little Conversations

One Sunday I went to the cathedral for Mass and chose the first narrow pew halfway up the side aisle. The position was perfect. I had a straight, unimpeded view of the sanctuary. As I complimented myself on this excellent seating choice, I said a rather flippant prayer, "So, Lord, when will a seven-foot tall man come in the pew in front of me?" Moments later, as the opening hymn began, my prayer was answered: a very tall man and his son took up positions directly in front of me in that very pew. They could have seen well from any pew, but they squished up against the edge by the aisle blocking my perfect view. What could I do but acknowledge how consoling it is that God hears our every prayer?

How often I have wished I were tall enough spiritually to overlook certain things, to be considerate of difference, patient with change, kindly, understanding, and accepting.

Anthony de Mello related this little gem: To a disciple forever complaining about others the Master said, "If it is peace you want, seek to change yourself, not other people. It is easier to protect your feet with slippers than to carpet the whole of the earth."[60]

I guess it's good advice for me, too, with all my little pet peeves. It makes me reflect again on my bread table conversation with Jesus.

We have a table in our dining room with two toasters, a plastic bin of bread, a few jelly jars, peanut butter, and, of course, real butter. There are little dishes for the used knives, but they have a way of jumping off and lying on the table amid the crumbs. When I took this on as my cleaning duty, I got very frustrated. I was merrily grumbling one morning when I heard the Lord ask me: "So, you're complaining again about the bread table." My response was something like, "Gulp!" He continued: "You should be grateful you have bread and something to put on it. Also, you don't have to eat alone. And, lastly, have you ever noticed the mess people make around my table of life?"

What could I possibly respond but to once again thank him for listening?

Do you have a pet peeve that could become a prayerful conversation? What would it sound like?

# 64

# Super-Duper Hero

The charitable person is able to see the good in his brethren. Everyone has good traits, as well as bad and defective traits. Where is there a man without fault? One who is very intelligent may talk too much. Another who is strong willed may be too hard on others. One who is good hearted may be too indulgent. To see good, means to regard a person for the good he does, instead of condemning him for the good he does not do.[61]

How easy it is to criticize others for what they don't do even more than for what they do that really is wrong. Personal wars and standoffs occur in families and between should-be friends because of an offense. Some of these are presumed and misinterpreted wrongs, perhaps never really communicated to the offender. There are real ones, too, unfortunately. We all have known or heard of folks who haven't spoken for years and some who won't even hear mention of the name of the other.

How we need to hear and take to heart this advice of the Pauline priest Blessed Timothy: "One of the surest signs of love toward our neighbor is the pardon of offenses. This becomes heroic when we try to save those who have offended us, and to benefit those who have done us evil."[62]

This makes me reflect that our fascination with superheroes is one more sign of our calling to heaven, to God. It is a universal enchantment, a dream of every person to be a hero someday, to discover in some unique way an inner strength at the moment of need, and we will save the day for others. No capes, no laser weapons, no flying, no bounding to heights, no extra strength or speed—only the intentions of the heart of Christ. This heroism is implanted in us at Baptism; we only have to implement it, to call it forth. We should always speak well of others, even when evil is spoken about us. This is the heroism of charity and, boy, is it difficult.

How would you judge your own heroism?

# 65

# Saints and Complaints

It has been said throughout these pages that I need to concentrate on being holy *as myself*, but holiness *is* Christ so I must strive "to put on Christ." We don't know a lot about what Christ was like, except what we can conclude from the Gospels: his words, actions, concerns, self-description. I must see, however, how I fit into this Christ. Also, I look to Paul who shows us what a Christian looks like, what it looks like to be Christ in our own self.

Does this seem too simple? We live in the age where everything is automatic, push-button, but for serious spiritual things we want a step-by-step formula—not too simple. Converting our complaints is a simple matter of the will. I *will* speak kindly. I *will* think kindly.

Blessed James Alberione says:

> One who does not love always finds reasons to grumble, but one who has genuine spiritual love always finds reasons to sympathize, to adapt to others, to pardon.[63]

Saints are people living Christ in themselves: "It is no longer I, but Christ who lives in me" (see Gal 2:20). "I have put on Christ" (see Rm 13:14). "I bear the brand marks of Christ in my body" (see Gal 6:17). These brand marks are the effects of love, of charity.

When we complain, it is because of confusion. It is an inner confusion that asks: who am I supposed to be? Am I supposed to be myself or what the moment dictates? What reaction should I give? What is expected of me?

I *am* a Christian—no argument there if I've been baptized. It is the one mark that doesn't come off. It is my new and eternal identity. So it means I am Christ. Saint Paul expressed what that should mean. It is not just a logo or a label or even a tattoo; it is the very essence of my being. I am a Christian man or Christian woman—a man or woman in Christ—he is my form. I look like him (as any good portrait of Christ that shows us in paint and canvas or as an actor what Christ would look like). I am Christ portrayed. I act like him; he looks like me. He has my mannerisms; I have his motivations.

God is love.
Jesus is God.
We are Jesus (Christians).
Therefore, we are to be love.

# 66

# Daily Challenge

*Nobody loves me; everybody hates me. I'm just gonna' eat some worms.*

This little ditty represents the ongoing theme of the classic complainer: *somebody done me wrong.* The unfortunate aspect of the complainer's theme is that they rarely find even a tiny part of the problem bearing their name. They are the victim, but never the perpetrator, and only occasionally a full partner in the daily tiff. Some would have been prosperous farmhands because they are great "pickers." Others, like old horses, are genuine "nags." Then there are those who simply drop hints all around, by which, of course, they don't mean *anything.*

Being so touchy while actually being the instigator of your own present pet peeve isn't a direct route to holiness. An about-face would be necessary to make the striving for holiness easier, but a total change of character is pretty unrealistic. So, what then? Perhaps the best approach is simply to be more attentive to life as it comes. What does that mean? Practice the needed virtue and pray, pray, pray. Examine your day—not just in the evening before sleep, but often during the day's events. Look carefully at what you complain about. Then play back your words. Forget what the other person involved said or did. You are interested in correcting yourself, not them. *What* did you say, *how* did you say it, and if you can figure it out, *why* did you say it. The next best step is to rehearse what you would have said if you could live that encounter again. Most important is to be gentle with yourself in this process—no ranting, no raving. Try to be nice to yourself.

Here is a little line to use as a continual reminder: "Abide patiently, forgive easily, understand mercifully, and forget utterly." Remember, just wanting to live this way won't make you a new person, but constantly working on being new every day (and praying for the grace you need) will make you holy. This is the lesson we learn from a fictional "saint" given to us by Louisa May Alcott. Her character, Marmee, the beloved mother of the four *Little Women,* has sage advise for her ever-impulsive daughter Jo who bemoans her terrible temper. Marmee confesses this was her challenge as well. She says, *Watch, pray, and keep struggling on.*[64] In other words, the best way to overcome our less-than-admirable defects is to soldier-on, that is, "fight the good fight" for patience, gentleness, kindness, mercy, etc.

# Characteristics of Charity

Paul, the great interpreter of "Christ living in me," has given us a formula for conversion in First Corinthians 13:1–13—the Characteristics of Charity. These descriptive characteristics are practical pointers for confronting our defects. As you go through the Apostle's list, look at each of them and plan ways to switch your negative energies for the positive energy of love. The Characteristics of Charity are a wonderful antidote to the habit of complaining.

> Charity is patient, is kind; charity does not envy, is not pretentious, is not puffed up, is not ambitious, is not self-seeking, is not provoked; thinks no evil, does not rejoice over wickedness, but rejoices with the truth; bears with all things, believes all things, hopes all things, endures all things.
>
> Charity never fails, whereas prophecies will disappear, and tongues will cease, and knowledge will be destroyed. For we know in part and we prophecy in part; but when that which is perfect has come, that which is imperfect will be done away with. When I was a child, I spoke as a child, I felt as a child, I thought as a child. Now that I have become a man, I have put away the things of a child. We see now through a mirror in an obscure manner, but then face to face.

Now I know in part, but then I shall know even as I have been known.

So there abide faith, hope and charity, these three; but the greatest of these is charity. (Confraternity translation, 1941)

## I. Charity is patient

What does it mean to a complainer to say that charity is patient?

We ask: "What is that person thinking? They have no consideration for another person's feelings or needs."

Saint Thérèse confided to a fellow sister that she was annoyed finding her things out of order one day when she returned to her painting.

> For instance: when starting to paint, if I find the brushes in disorder, and a ruler or penknife gone, I feel inclined to lose patience, and have to keep a firm hold over myself not to betray my feelings.[65]

Saint Francis de Sales offers us a panorama of the exercise of patience.

> That patience with the idiosyncrasies of another, that bearing with the clownish and troublesome actions and ways of our neighbor, those victories over our own moods and passions, those mortifications of our lesser inclinations, that effort against our aversions and repugnances, that heartfelt and sweet acknowledgment of our own imperfections, the continual pains we take to keep our souls in equanimity, that love of our littleness, that gentle and gracious welcome we give to the contempt and censure of our condition, of

our life, of our conversation, of our actions. . . . Theotimus, all these things are more profitable to our souls than we can conceive, if heavenly love has the management of them.[66]

## II. Charity is kind

What is the meaning of the word "kind?" We say: "I'll treat you *in kind*," or "You are a *kindred* spirit, but he is one *of a kind*." A kind person is good, benevolent, considerate, gracious, and gentle. The dictionary offers as an antonym the word cruel. When we think of a complaint, it would certainly tip the balance toward cruel as opposed to all the positive synonyms.

According to Blessed James Alberione, all that is necessary to understand kindness is to look at Jesus in the Gospels because "every word, every action of the Master contains a special grace that enables the practice of the virtue about which they are reading."[67]

> We would never have understood what humility is, or meekness, patient bearing of wrongs, virginity and fraternal charity practiced to the point of self-immolation, if we had not read and meditated on the examples and teachings of Our Lord on these virtues.[68]

John Randal Bradburne (1921–1979) took this imitation of Christ quite literally. As a convert to Catholicism following his military service, John found his spiritual home as a Third Order Franciscan. His life dream was threefold: to serve lepers, to wear the Franciscan habit, and to die a martyr. Perhaps too idealistic for many, but Jesus took John's dream seriously. John's quest for a way to live out his Christian vocation took him to a leper colony in Zimbabwe. When civil war broke out, he refused to abandon these people despite the danger to himself, and eventually was abducted and murdered. At his funeral a pool of blood formed under his coffin. The source could not be found, but upon investigation it was discovered that he was being buried without his Franciscan habit. And so, John Bradburne, who modeled his life on the gentle, loving life of Jesus, had his three wishes fulfilled. His cause for canonization has been opened.

## III. Charity does not envy

Why do others get better gifts? Why can't we all get the same things? This complaint applies to actual things, the gifts we give one another, and the gifts of nature and grace that differ so much in each of us. We all have the tendency to compare *and* to stare at what the other one has.

Envy is a rather ugly word, and we usually try to hide the evidence from others. *Heaven forbid anyone thinks I'm envious!* Being envious is acted out in jealousy. This is a special problem for children, who want everything to be fair, and it is particularly unattractive in adults.

Jesus compares the kingdom to a landowner who hires a series of day-laborers to work in his vineyard. He picks up these men at all different hours of the working day, so at the end of the day when he hands out the pay, the workers have certain expectations. He starts by paying the last hired hand a full day's pay, so the early workers envision a bigger haul. They too are given a day's wage and nothing more. Crazy, right? They thought so, too, and complained. The owner of the vineyard calls them out for this. They agreed on an amount and that's what he has given. "Can't I do what I want with what's mine? Or are you jealous because I'm generous?" (Mt 20:1–16 TNT). The landowner, who is God, is crazy generous!

While we do try to hide any jealous feelings, others can often see envy in our eyes, or hear it in our snide remarks. The classic example of the effects of jealousy and envy is found as Saul and David return to Israel after triumphing over the Philistines. The women stream out playing tambourines and singing: "Saul has killed his thousands, and David his ten thousands" (1 Sam 18:7). King Saul was furious that David received higher praise; after all, wasn't Saul the greater? "What more can he have but the kingdom?" Saul complained. Read about their tumultuous relationship in 1 Samuel. One heart was ruled by jealousy, the other by devotion.

## IV. Love is not pretentious

Just as it says, the complainer *pretends* to be better and to see more. The pretender doesn't love, and the love he is looking for is only admiration.

Many clerics dealing with foundresses of religious orders could have been categorized as pretentious. One example would be Saint Julie Billiart's constant difficulty with priests who assumed control of the nascent Sisters of Notre Dame that she had founded. She concluded at one point: "The good God must have some hidden design in all this, for everything to be so disturbed without reason."[69]

This form of complaint pops up very noticeably in the Gospel, too, following right after the generous landowner. This time the mother of Zebedee's sons, James and John, approaches with her boys to ask for a rather pretentious favor. She kneels down and presents her case, "Say that these two sons of mine can sit, one at your right hand and one at your left hand, in your Kingdom" (Mt 20:20–26 TNT). If Jesus' reply sounds a little rattled, it's because two verses before this he explained that he is going to Jerusalem to be condemned—mocked, scourged, and crucified (and to rise on the third day). "You don't know what you're asking for!"

When we complain in pretense, that we should be considered more important than we are, we waste our potential to be more authentic.

## V. Love is not puffed up

"Puffed up" comes next because if pretension isn't checked by reality, we can become proud.

A complainer is often arrogant. It is almost impossible for such a one to restrain from bursting forth in praise of self. Here is where the saintly potential complainers shine. Their specialty is humility. Saint Bernadette Soubirous gave an outstanding example of this humility. "She put up submissively with being reprimanded in public and more frequently than was her share. 'The Mistress is quite right,' she confided . . . , 'for I have a great deal of pride.'"[70]

Saint Basil tells us: "It seems that self-knowledge is the most important of all things. For not only does the eye that is taken up with outward things fail to turn its glance inwardly, but even our very mind, while swift to note another's fault, is slow at seeing its own defects."[71]

## VI. Love is not ambitious

A person given to complaining is always looking for an opportunity to get the upper hand or to get ahead of others.

Before his appointment as Archbishop of Canterbury, Saint Thomas Becket was chancellor for King Henry II; both were very ambitious men. Thomas' submission to the grace of his ordination, however, made him a true servant of God much to the disappointment of the king. Henry was counting on Thomas to give him control of the Church. In the end Saint Thomas Becket became victim of a complaint that got him assassinated. In a fit of anger the king complained, "Is there no one to free me from this bothersome priest?" A group of knights immediately rode off and killed the archbishop in his cathedral.

The only ambition love should have is to love more. The ways of showing love are countless, the opportunities are constant.

## VII. Love is not self-seeking

Complainers are over-achievers. When their great plans are thwarted, they are piqued. A former priest had served well as a missionary for several years, but when his plans for evangelization were not accepted by his bishop, he left the priesthood in protest. He appeared to be overly attached to his own way of doing good, and who isn't guilty of this from time to time.

How often our service of God is heavily colored by our desires and inclinations. But love should always be directed outward, first toward God and then toward our neighbors. We always exaggerate our needs, but the more this happens the more closed in on ourselves we become.

We rarely think of the good we do for ourselves as a sacrifice; it only seems a burden when done for others. Mother Paula Cordero, the first Daughter of Saint Paul in the United States, told us: "The sacrifice of being charitable is not a sacrifice; it is a duty, it is a must."

We could stop a moment to thank God for all the hidden saints, those we don't notice in our lifetime and those who go into history as unremarkable except in the eyes of God. These holy people were saintly in simple ways, for the most part. They didn't seek any acclaim. Of course, they all had faults; they had complaints, and perhaps sins, but they made their way toward God. They sought him in their weakness and their strength as we, too, must do.

## VIII. Charity is not provoked

Saint Augustine explains this very plainly:

"Learn," [Jesus] says, "from me"; not how to manufacture a world and create various natures; nor even those other things which he achieved here, hiddenly as God, manifestly as man. He doesn't mean them either: nor does he say, "Learn of me to expel fevers from the sick, to put devils to flight, to raise the dead, to command the winds and the waves, to walk upon the waters." No. Neither does he say, "Learn these of me." These things he gave to some of his disciples, to others he didn't give them: but this, "Learn of me," he said to all; from this precept let no one excuse himself. "Learn of me for I am meek and humble of heart."[72]

Provocation is not effective over the self-possessed. Blessed James Alberione points out:

Personality is neither emancipation nor independence, but complete control over self. It is in obedience and self denial that one best expresses his own personality. The more one obeys, the freer he becomes, and the more he masters himself. This self-dominion is perfect balance—genuine personality.[73]

Even someone as revered as Saint Bernadette was frequently reprimanded in public. This definitely provoked her. "I'm seething inside, but they don't see what's going on there," she admitted to Sister Marthe du Rais. "There would be no merit if one did not master oneself."[74]

Another example of such self-dominion was given by Saint Mary MacKillop of Australia (1842–1909). She was accused of mismanaging her fledgling religious community, of insubordination to Church authorities, and was summarily excommunicated. She sternly warned her sisters not to complain or oppose the unjust censure placed on her by the bishop. She would not tolerate complaints.

This is how holy ones do complaints.

# IX. Charity thinks no evil

A complainer *does* think evil but will always deny it.

In her commentary on this characteristic of charity, Sister Nazarene Morando explains:

> Should they see someone perform a good deed, they immediately think that it was done for selfish reasons. They are inclined to see everything through dark glasses, giving an evil interpretation even to what is good. They are gloomy characters whose unbridled imagination is the cause of much suffering both to them and to others. They proudly claim to know men through and through and to be undeceived, as are "simpletons and the ignorant," by mere appearances, by what they call "pure imitation of virtue."
>
> By acting this way, however, they only show what they themselves are. The ease with which they judge, suspect, and believe evil of others is a result of the ease with which they commit evil. It is not up to vice to judge virtue, as it is not the duty of darkness to judge light or of error to judge the truth.[75]

Here is a further explanation of this characteristic by the well-respected spiritual author, Hubert Van Zeller:

> The act of compassion is, whatever the manner of its expression, primarily an interior one. It may show itself in any one of the corporal works of mercy, but before it brings the particular kind of relief which the situation demands it has to exist in the mind. Otherwise the acts might well be acts of vainglory. So much does it reside in the mind rather than in the performance that sometimes compassion does not have to show itself outwardly at all. It is simply there—waiting.[76]

# X. Charity doesn't rejoice over wickedness (injustice)

A complainer delights in the smoke and mirrors he or she uses to disguise falsehood. They find justification in the wickedness of others. When offended, they want to pay tit for tat.

Saint Paul instead teaches us:

> Let no bad word come from your mouths; instead, say only what is necessary and will serve to edify, so that those who hear may receive grace. . . . Let all bitterness, anger, wrath, angry shouting, and slander be put away from you, along with all malice. Be kind to one another, compassionate, forgiving each other just as God forgave you in Christ (Eph 4:29–32 TNT).

How does a Christian deal with this injustice when they can see a way out for themselves? Our example is Saint Margaret Clitherow (c. 1553–1586), a butcher's wife from Elizabethan England. She was accused of harboring traitors (priests) in her home. She refused to enter a plea because she didn't believe she had done anything worthy of punishment. The prosecutors then tried to accuse her of infidelity to her husband. But he wouldn't believe anything said against her. To him she was the best wife in all of England, and the best Catholic as well. By not declaring before the jury, Margaret was condemned by the state. From prison she admitted to friends that her reticence to complain or excuse herself was due in part to spare her family, especially her children, and her servants the sorrow of being forced to testify against her. She wanted the guilt over her death to fall on as few people as possible.

## XI. Charity rejoices with the truth

Who better to give us his take on the joy of truth than Saint Paul?

> Whatever is true, whatever is honorable, whatever is just, whatever is pure, whatever is pleasing, whatever is gracious, if there is any excellence or anything praiseworthy, think of these things. (Phil 4:8 TNT)

So, if we want to develop a Christian personality, we have to reproduce the whole Christ in ourselves; we have to believe in his word, follow his examples and live his life:

> [U]ntil we all attain to unity of faith and knowledge of the Son of God to mature manhood, to the extent of Christ's full stature. Thus we'll no longer be infants, tossed and carried here and there by every wind of teaching coming from human cunning, from their craftiness in developing deceitful schemes. Instead by speaking the truth in love we'll grow in every way into him—Christ—who is the head upon whom the whole body depends (Eph 4:13–15 TNT).

Who could we say rejoiced in the truth more than Blessed Victoria Rasoamanarivo (1848–1894) of Madagascar? When the priests were banished from the kingdom, Victoria, a member of the royal family and a recent convert, took it upon herself to keep the faith alive. She stood up to the guards who tried to keep Catholics from Sunday worship. "If you must shed blood, begin with mine; but fear will not keep us from gathering for prayer," she boldly proclaimed. Victoria devised ways to communicate between the Catholic communities; she catechized and cared for the poor. Rather than complain about the impediments to the practice of the faith, Blessed Victoria set out to make it possible in a hostile environment.

## XII. Charity bears all things

Charity bears all things whereas complainers only bear what is their own choice.

In speaking of the possibilities of apostolic works that are available to us, Blessed James Alberione suggests prayer and physical, moral, and interior suffering.

> Do not think you are wasting time when you have to suffer. Welcome, bear with, and offer up annoyance, sickness, sorrow, obscurity, desolation and whatever else troubles, opposes, or contradicts you. Bring it all to Jesus, not only as a means of purification but as an apostolate.[77]

Along with that suggestion, we can add this succinct version by the ancient Greek philosopher Epictetus: "The two powers which, in my opinion, constitute a wise man are those of bearing and forbearing."

One such wise man was Venerable Cardinal Francis Xavier Nguyen Van Thuan (1928–2002). Six days after being appointed Coadjutor Archbishop of Saigon, Bishop Van Thuan was arrested because he was a religious leader and because he was the nephew of the deposed prime minister. His arrest led to thirteen years of imprisonment, nine of which were spent in solitary confinement. Although he couldn't attend to his flock, he found ways to smuggle out scraps of paper on which he wrote prayers and encouraging thoughts for the faithful. One such prayer reads:

I'm happy here in this cell, where white mushrooms are growing on my sleeping mat, because you are with me, because you want me to live here with you. I have spoken much in my lifetime; now I speak no more. It is your turn to speak to me, Jesus; I am listening to you.[78]

## XIII. Charity believes all

Charity believes all things, whereas complainers thrive on the possibility that another is in error or, in fact, lying.

Blessed James Alberione offers us some thoughts about this:

— "Ideas influence judgment, judgment excites sentiment, sentiment determines internal and external acts."[79]

— "A saint is not one who is worn-out, an irresponsible person who cannot make up his mind to do his share in life. For Saint Paul, sanctity is the full maturity of man, 'perfect manhood'" (see Eph 4:13).

— "The saint does not wrap himself up in himself; he opens himself up to development. He does not stay still; rather his motto is growth and progress. Sanctity is life, movement, nobility, dynamic enthusiasm—not the kind that falls off but the good kind that keeps rising upward! But sanctity will be only and always in proportion to the spirit of faith and to will power. God is with us! We cooperate with him."[80]

Father Alberione himself epitomizes love that believes all— not just all the truths taught by our faith, but all the things God inspired him to do. When he was only sixteen years old, he was inspired to meet head on the challenges of the twentieth century. He would combat the influence of the bad press with the apostolate of the good press. Despite every challenge, Alberione prepared a vast religious family (the Pauline Family) to flood the world with God's Word, to enlighten and direct great projects for God's glory and for the good of God's people. All this notwithstanding his own fragile health, constant misunderstanding, criticism, opposition, and lack of funds.

# XIV. Charity hopes all things

One prone to complaint hopes only that his or her suspicions are accurate. Instead, someone who is working to be charitable hopes that all is trending upward. They really hope that others have the best of intentions even if some mistakes have been made. Hope is the virtue that motivates charity.

When Our Lady appears in a locale and leaves a reminder of her Son's desires for us, or rebukes a wrongdoing, she always offers hope. She speaks of the Lord's love and mercy and of the reward of heaven.

Let us learn to "hope against hope" (see Rm 4:18), as Saint Paul counsels us. Paul is referring to Abraham who had this unflinching hope in God's promise to make him father of many nations, even though he was an old man with no children. So should our love be sustained by hope. One of the most demanding love/hope relationships we must foster is toward the Church. Our love for the Church should sustain our hope for her future through scandal and indifference, persecution and prosperity. This love and hope are in Jesus' promise to be with his Church, that is, with us, until the end of the world (Mt 28:20).

Consider someone like Blessed Miguel Pro (1891–1927), a Jesuit priest who worked clandestinely to serve and preserve the Catholic faith in Mexico during the persecution. He was constantly on the run, assuming very creative disguises to elude those bent on apprehending him. His faith was in the promise of Jesus for his Church, which was confirmed by the apparition of our Lady of Guadalupe. Father Pro brought people the sacraments with a very optimistic and cheerful demeanor, hoping to keep the practice of the faith alive despite the malice of the Church's enemies. When arrested, Father Pro was condemned on false charges without a trial and brought before a firing squad. He refused the blindfold offered him and faced the guns without flinching, his arms held in the form of the cross. His final words were, *"Viva Cristo Rey!"* "Long live Christ the King!"

## XV. Charity endures all things

The highpoint of holiness is precisely when we willingly suffer for another. This is the ultimate imitation of Christ, who endured not only all that his passion entailed, but also the misunderstandings, conflicts, and betrayals of his public ministry. Unfortunately, for the chronic complainer to endure anything silently, generously, courageously, is almost impossible (and seems unwarranted).

In a letter to her brother, Jean-Marie, in 1876, soon after he was discharged from the army, Saint Bernadette advised him to remember his Christian duty to live well his faith.

I know that soldiers have a lot to put up with, and have to do so without protest. If when they got up they were to say to our Lord every morning this short sentence: *My God, I wish to do and to endure everything today for love of you,* they would store up immeasurable treasure in heaven! If a soldier did that and performed his Christian duties as faithfully as possible, he would earn the same reward as any monk in a cloister![81]

What Saint Bernadette is explaining to Jean-Marie, we recognize as the Morning Offering. As children we learned this prayer in order to offer Jesus all our "prayers, actions, joys, and sufferings of this day" so that everything will be an act of love. Repetition helps us form this valuable habit and reduces the occasions of complaint.

## XVI. Reading from First Corinthians

Let us meditate on the words that follow in the reading from 1 Corinthians and notice how they speak to those of us who are given to complaining.

> Love never ends; as for prophecies, they will pass away; as for tongues, they will cease; as for knowledge, it will pass away. For our knowledge is imperfect and our prophecy is imperfect; but when the perfect comes, the imperfect will pass away. When I was a child, I spoke like a child, I thought like a child, I reasoned like a child; when I became a man, I gave up childish ways. For now I see in a mirror dimly, but then face to face. Now I know in part; then I shall understand fully, even as I have been fully understood. So faith, hope, love abide, these three; but the greatest of these is love. (1 Cor 13:8–13 RSV)

Love, the motivation for any type of charity, is the one lasting quality of life, simply because God himself is love itself. We complainers consider ourselves prophets who can discern and interpret the words, actions, and motivations of others. I am operating out of a childish model because I am not yet fully mature in Christ. I speak as a child, think as a child, reason as a child, *and* complain as a child.

Saint Francis de Sales tells us to be *calm, cool, and collected* when dealing with ourselves. Take time to reflect on his words. He offers the secret formula for overcoming whatever defect we struggle with. His words reflect on the description of true self-love that Saint Paul gives when he outlined the characteristics of charity.

> To live in a gentle way, it is important to respect ourselves, never growing irritated with ourselves or our imperfections. Although it is but reasonable that we should be displeased and grieved at our own faults, we need to guard against being bitter, angry, or fretful about them. Many people fall into the error of being angry because they have been angry, or impatient because they have given way to impatience; this keeps them in a chronic state of irritation, strengthens the impressions made, and prepares one for a fresh fall on the first occasion. Moreover, all this anger and irritation against one's self fosters pride, springing as it does from self-love, which is disturbed and upset by its own imperfection.
>
> What we need is a quiet, steady, firm displeasure at our own faults.
>
> So then, when you have fallen, lift up your heart quietly, humbling yourself deeply before God for your frailty,

without marveling that you fell, since there is no cause to marvel because weakness is weak, infirmity, infirm, and frailty, frail. Sincerely regret that you should have offended God, and begin anew to seek the grace you need, with a deep trust in God's mercy, and with a bold, brave heart.[82]

These Characteristics of Charity show us the various ways to sanctify our tendency to complain about everything. Love is multifaceted and so it contains the antidote for every negative impulse of our hearts. I suggest that we go back over these Characteristics of Charity and try to find experiences from our own lives that fit with each. Thank the Lord for what we see as living love, and let us bless what we discover in ourselves that needs to be converted to Christ. We should pray over our weaknesses and offer them to God, asking help to overcome them, but also to see in them the means to humility that is the safeguard of all our virtues.

# Postscript

Some chapters ago I mentioned my infatuation with Saint Thérèse. I don't remember if this incident I am about to relate came before or after my conversation with my father when he told me to find another model; however, this is what happened. As I said, I was very much into imitating the Little Flower, and I even got a piece of driftwood to kneel on in my bedroom. It was very uncomfortable, by the way, but I persevered for a while. During one of these prayer experiences God spoke, as he is want to do, within the prayer itself. This is not a mystical extravaganza as we find in movies, but just God within the context of the prayer. Noting my interest in prayer, God asked me if I was willing to give him what Thérèse had given. That stopped me for a moment in my pious reverie, and I answered, "No, not yet." My answer may have startled me more than his question did. There was no divine gasp, no heavy thud of a door closing, nothing dramatic. God just let me go on being the teenager me, and he went on being his usual loving, providential Self. I can tell God wasn't shaken by my response because he still called me to follow him as a religious—which I did and have lived happily ever after. I must relate, however, that for years into my life as a religious I wondered about my "no." What would have happened had I said "yes"? Would my life have been any different? There is no way of knowing; but I do know that it led me to believe very strongly in God's interest in each of us. In retrospect it helped me realize God was saying that he already had a Saint Thérèse and now he wanted to show me my own path to holiness. It would not be as short or direct as that of Thérèse. I didn't have her early formation, or her firmness of character, but that is fine. I was not meant to follow her mold, but to let myself, with all my personal qualities and quirks, be molded into a unique image of Christ. And here I stand so many years later and some of the quirks can still be seen sticking up through the budding virtues.

Look at your own life with Christ. Try to trace out how he has led you to the present. Thank God for the many graced moments, humble yourself for the times you failed, and ask his pleasure to continue leading you on.

> "Don't desire not to be what you are, but desire to be very well what you are."
>
> —Saint Francis de Sales

# Notes

1. James Alberione, *"For Me to Live Is Christ"* (Boston: St. Paul Editions, 1984), 40 [private use].

2. Lewis Carroll, *Through the Looking Glass and What Alice Found There* (London: MacMillan & Co., 1872), 124.

3. John Henry Newman, *An Essay on the Development of Christian Doctrine* (London, New York, Bombay, and Calcutta: Longmans, Green, and Co., 1909), 33.

4. Saint Antony the Abbot (c. 251–356).

5. See Mary Margaret Funk, *Thoughts Matter: The Practice of the Spiritual Life* (New York: Continuum 2005), 67.

6. Mother Thecla Merlo, FSP, Conferences IV, 34–35 (private use).

7. Dom John Chapman, *The Spiritual Letters of Dom John Chapman, OSB* (London: Sheed & Ward, 1946), 156.

8. Frank J. Sheed, *Theology and Sanity* (London: Sheed & Ward, 1946/1978), 323.

9. Ibid.

10. Ana Carrigan, *Salvador Witness: The Life and Calling of Jean Donovan* (New York: Simon and Schuster, 1984), 99.

11. Ibid., 162.

12. Teresa of Ávila, *Life of Saint Teresa*, First American Edition, trans. John Dalton (Philadelphia: P. F. Cunningham 186-?), 345–6 (adapted).

13. Ibid., 259 (adapted).

14. Thérèse, de Lisieux, *The Story of a Soul (L'Histoire d'une Âme): The*

*Autobiography of St. Thérèse of Lisieux with Additional Writings and Sayings of St. Thérèse*, trans. Thomas N. Taylor (London: Burns, Oates & Washbourne 191-?), Chapter X. http://www.gutenberg.org/cache/epub/16772/pg16772-images.html.

15. Pope Francis, *On the Call to Holiness in Today's World: Gaudete et Exsultate* (Boston: Pauline Books & Media, 2018), 45.

16. Thérèse, de Lisieux, *The Story of a Soul*, Chapter X.

17. Ibid., 297.

18. St. Thérèse of Lisieux, *Spirit of St. Thérèse*, compiled by the Carmelites of Lisieux (London: Burns and Oates, 1948), 179.

19. Kathryn Spink, *Mother Teresa: An Authorized Biography*, revised and updated (New York: HarperOne, 2011), 13.

20. Brian Kolodiejchuk, MC, editor and commentary, *Mother Teresa Come Be My Light: The Private Writings of the "Saint of Calcutta"* (New York: Doubleday, 2007), 169.

21. Ibid., 189.

22. Mother Teresa of Calcutta, *A Gift for God: Prayers and Meditations* (San Francisco: Harper & Row, Publishers, 1975), 58.

23. Philip Schaff, ed., *A Select Library of the Nicene and Post-Nicene Fathers of the Christian Church*, vol. 6 (Buffalo: The Christian Literature Co., 1890–1900), 172 (adapted).

24. Schaff, *Nicene and Post-Nicene Fathers*, 87 (adapted).

25. Ibid., 487–8 (adapted).

26. Ibid., 251 (adapted).

27. Ibid., 181 (adapted).

28. Blessed James Alberione, *Paul the Apostle: Inspiration and Model* (Rome: Society of St. Paul, 2008), 28.

29. Robert Louis Stevenson, Father Damien—*An Open Letter to the Reverend Dr. Hyde of Honolulu*, *The Works of Robert Louis Stevenson*, vol. 15 (London: W. Heinemann in association with Chatto and Windus, Cassell and Longmans, Green, 1922), 479–501.

30. Vital Jourdain, SS.CC., *The Heart of Father Damien* (Milwaukee: The Bruce Publishing Company, 1955), 328.

31. Sister Maria Faustina Kowalska, *Divine Mercy in My Soul* [The Diary of the Servant of God, 151] (Stockbridge: Marian Press, 1987), 85.

32. Ibid., 1148, 421.

33. Evelyn Underhill, *Quotes for the Journey: Wisdom for the Way*, compiled by Gordon S. Jackson (Colorado Springs: NavPress, 2000), 22.

34. Caryll Houselander, *Guilt* (New York: Sheed & Ward, 1951), 129.

35. Cf. Alban Goodier, *Saints for Sinners* (London: Sheed & Ward, 1930/1979), 92.

36. Maria Di Lorenzo, *Blessed Pier Giorgio Frassati: An Ordinary Christian* (Boston: Pauline Books & Media, 2004), 85.

37. Catherine of Siena, *Saint Catherine of Siena as Seen in Her Letters*, trans. & ed. Vida D. Scudder (London, J. M. Dent; New York, E. P. Dutton, 1905), 234 (adapted).

38. Blessed Raymond of Capua, *Life of St. Catherine of Siena*, trans. (New York: Lamb, Kennedy & Sons, 1960, 220.

39. Letter to Sister Daniella, in Catherine of Siena, *Saint Catherine of Siena*, 58 (adapted).

40. Gertrude, The Great, *The Life and Revelations of Saint Gertrude, Virgin and Abbess, of the Order of St. Benedict* (London : Burns & Oates; New York : Benziger, 187-), 288.

41. Blessed James Alberione, *"I Was Created to Love God"* (Boston: St. Paul Editions, 1980), 43 (for private use only).

42. Ibid., 33.

43. Ibid., 34.

44. Ibid., 68.

45. Ibid., 70.

46. George Herbert, *The Poems of George Herbert* (London: Oxford University Press 1907), 177.

47. Mother Thecla Merlo, FSP, Conferences, vol. 3, 20–21 (private use).

48. Blessed James Alberione, *Mi protendo in Avanti* (Alba E.P., 1954), 276, and *Ut Perfectus Sit Homo Dei* (Rome: SSP, 1998), 223–224.

49. The *Didache* 3:6–8.

50. Dorothy Day, *Dorothy Day: Selected Writings*, ed. Robert Ellsberg (Maryknoll, NY: Orbis Books 2011/1983), 70.

51. Dorothy Day, *Meditations: Dorothy Day* (New York: Paulist Press, 1970), 53–54.

52. Gemma Oberto, *Mother Scholastica Rivata: Joy in God's Service* (Bangalore: St. Paul Publications, 2008), 41.

53. C. S. Lewis, *Mere Christianity* (San Francisco: HarperSanFrancisco, 2001/1952), 7.

54. Dom John Chapman, *The Spiritual Letters of Dom John Chapman, OSB* (London: Sheed & Ward, 1946), 152.

55. St. Thérèse of Lisieux, *Story of a Soul: The Autobiography of St. Thérèse of Lisieux,* 3rd ed. translated from the Original Manuscripts (Washington, DC: ICS Publications, 1997), 127.

56. See *Little Flowers of St. Francis of Assisi,* paraphrase of no. 34 (Boston: St. Paul Editions, 1976), 125.

57. Thomas à Kempis, *The Imitation of Christ* (Boston: Pauline Books & Media, 2015), 62.

58. Ibid., 41.

59. Blessed James Alberione, *Insights Into Religious Life* (Boston: St. Paul Editions, 1977), 52–54.

60. Anthony de Mello, SJ, *One Minute Wisdom* (Garden City, NY: Doubleday & Company, Inc., 1986), 38.

61. Blessed Timothy Giaccardo, SSP, *Look Heavenward* (Derby, NY: St. Paul Publications, 1962), 48.

62. Ibid., 47.

63. Alberione, 567.

64. See Louisa May Alcott, *Little Women*, chapter 8.

65. Thérèse, de Lisieux, *The Story of a Soul,* Chapter IX.

66. St. Francis de Sales, excerpt from *Treatise on the Love of God*, Book 12, chap. 6, as found in *Courage in Chaos: Wisdom from St. Francis de Sales* (Boston: Pauline Books & Media, 2012), 38.

67. Blessed James Alberione, *Personality and Configuration with Christ* (Boston: St. Paul Editions, 1967), 77.

68. Ibid., 76.

69. Roseanne Murphy, SND de N, *Julie Billiart: Woman of Courage* (New York/Mahwah, NJ: Paulist Press, 1995), 90.

70. Abbe Francois Trochu, *Saint Bernadette Soubirous* (Charlotte: TAN Books, 1957), 284.

71. Saint Basil, *The Sunday Sermons of the Great Fathers,* vol. 3, trans. and ed. M. F. Toal (Chicago: Henry Regnery Co., 1959), 87.

72. Augustine, Bishop of Hippo, *Sermons on Selected Lessons of the New Testament* (Oxford: John Henry Parker; London: J. and F. Rivington, 1854), 829.

73. Alberione, *Personality and Configuration with Christ*, 172–173.

74. Trochu, *Saint Bernadette Soubirous*, 284–285.

75. Sister Nazarene Morando, FSP, *The Characteristics of Charity* (Boston: St. Paul Editions, 1963), 64–65.

76. Hubert Van Zeller, OSB, *Approach to Calvary* (New York: Sheed & Ward, 1961), 35.

77. Alberione, *Personality and Configuration with Christ,* 182.

78. Francis Xavier NguyenVan Thuan, *Five Loaves and Two Fish* (Boston: Pauline Books & Media, 1997), 43.

79. Alberione, *Personality and Configuration with Christ*, 49.

80. Ibid., 40.

81. John Cumming, ed., *Letters from Saints to Sinners* (New York: A Crossroad Book, The Crossroad Publishing Company, 1996; first published in Kent, Great Britain: Burns & Oates, 1996), 57.

82. Francis de Sales, excerpt from *Introduction to the Devout Life*, Part 3, chap. 9, in *Courage in Chaos: Wisdom from St. Francis de Sales* (Boston: Pauline Books & Media, 2012), 13.

# Also by Sr. Mary Lea Hill, FSP:

### Prayer and You

Wit and Wisdom from a Crabby Mystic

Short chapters that make prayer approachable for both those new to prayer and veterans. This book is a nudge in the right direction, offering countless examples of when, where, why, and how to pray.

0-8198-5999-0
$14.95
paperback, 192 pages

### Blessed Are the Stressed

Secrets to a Happy Heart
from a Crabby Mystic

How can we find true happiness in our often complicated and stressful lives? Let the Crabby Mystic show you how blessed are the stressed, grouchy, and grumpy—for they too can learn the secrets of a happy heart!

0-8198-1229-3
$14.95
paperback, 192 pages

BOOKS & MEDIA

A mission of the Daughters of St. Paul

As apostles of Jesus Christ, evangelizing today's world:

We are CALLED to holiness
by God's living Word and Eucharist.

We COMMUNICATE the Gospel message
through our lives and through all
available forms of media.

We SERVE the Church
by responding to the hopes and needs
of all people with the Word of God,
in the spirit of St. Paul.

For more information visit us at
www.pauline.org.

## BOOKS & MEDIA

The Daughters of St. Paul operate book and media centers at the following addresses. Visit, call, or write the one nearest you today, or find us at www.paulinestore.org.

CALIFORNIA
3908 Sepulveda Blvd, Culver City, CA 90230     310-397-8676
3250 Middlefield Road, Menlo Park, CA 94025     650-562-7060

FLORIDA
145 S.W. 107th Avenue, Miami, FL 33174     305-559-6715

HAWAII
1143 Bishop Street, Honolulu, HI 96813     808-521-2731

ILLINOIS
172 North Michigan Avenue, Chicago, IL 60601     312-346-4228

LOUISIANA
4403 Veterans Memorial Blvd, Metairie, LA 70006     504-887-7631

MASSACHUSETTS
885 Providence Hwy, Dedham, MA 02026     781-326-5385

MISSOURI
9804 Watson Road, St. Louis, MO 63126     314-965-3512

NEW YORK
115 E. 29th Street, New York City, NY 10016     212-754-1110

SOUTH CAROLINA
243 King Street, Charleston, SC 29401     843-577-0175

VIRGINIA
1025 King Street, Alexandria, VA 22314     703-549-3806

CANADA
3022 Dufferin Street, Toronto, ON M6B 3T5     416-781-9131